This is not just another book on male and female differences. Yes, it's practical, humorous, and a fun read. You'll see yourself and others through new eyes. You'll learn some new ways to give and receive love. But the most valuable feature is the section on spiritual intimacy. It alone is worth the price of the book. Really! This is a book you'll give to friends and want to read more than once.

GARY J. OLIVER, TH.M., PH.D.
Executive director of The Center for Healthy Relationships, professor of psychology and practical theology at John Brown University, and author of more than twenty books, including *Mad about Us* and *It's Okay to Be Angry*

In *Men Are Clams, Women Are Crowbars*, Dr. David Clarke's fresh, relevant, and humorous approach to gender differences will hit you right where you are in your own marriage. This book is sure to open the door to deeper understanding and better communication. A must read!

DAVID AND CLAUDIA ARP
Cofounders of Marriage Alive and authors of *10 Great Dates*

Refreshing, delightful, funny, practical—and *life-changing*! *Men Are Clams, Women Are Crowbars* is a must read. Regardless of how long a couple has been married, there is one thing this book can do for their marriage—improve it! A lot of books describe how to improve your marriage, but few really show you how to apply those principles practically and biblically. Clarke's book does so masterfully. *Men Are Clams, Women Are Crowbars* is a winner.

DR. RODNEY COOPER
Kenneth and Jean Hansen Professor of Discipleship and Leadership Development at Gordon-Conwell Theological Seminary, former national director of Promise Keepers, and nationally known speaker and author

Men Are Clams, Women Are Crowbars

Men Are
CLAMS

Women Are
CROWBARS

The Dos and Don'ts of
Getting Your Man to Open Up

David E. Clarke, Ph.D.
with William G. Clarke, M.A.

TYNDALE HOUSE PUBLISHERS, INC.
CAROL STREAM, ILLINOIS

FOCUS ON THE FAMILY® | FOCUS ON MARRIAGE™

Men Are Clams, Women Are Crowbars: The Dos and Don'ts of Getting Your Man to Open Up

© 2019 by David E. Clarke, Ph.D. All rights reserved.

A Focus on the Family book published by Tyndale House Publishers, Inc., Carol Stream, Illinois 60188

Focus on the Family and the accompanying logo and design are federally registered trademarks of Focus on the Family, 8605 Explorer Drive, Colorado Springs, CO 80920.

TYNDALE and Tyndale's quill logo are registered trademarks of Tyndale House Publishers, Inc.

All Scripture quotations, unless otherwise marked, are from *The Holy Bible, English Standard Version.* Copyright © 2001 by CrosswayBibles, a publishing ministry of Good News Publishers. Used by permission. All rights reserved.

People's names and certain details of their stories have been changed to protect the privacy of the individuals involved. However, the facts of what happened and the underlying principles have been conveyed as accurately as possible.

The use of material from or references to various websites does not imply endorsement of those sites in their entirety. Availability of websites and pages is subject to change without notice.

Editors: Larry Weeden and Kathy Davis
Cover design by Nathan Cook

Cover photograph of scallop copyright © chengyuzheng/iStockphoto. All rights reserved.
Cover photograph of clam copyright © 3drenderings/iStockphoto. All rights reserved.
Cover photograph of crowbar copyright © Björn Forenius/iStockphoto. All rights reserved.
Cover photograph of umbrella by Michael Fomkin on Pixabay.com.
Cover photograph of beach by Public Domain Pictures on Pexels.com.

This author is represented by Hartline Literary Agency, 123 Queenston Dr., Pittsburgh, PA 15235.

For information about special discounts for bulk purchases, please contact Tyndale House Publishers at csresponse@tyndale.com, or call 1-800-323-9400.

ISBN 978-1-58997-975-8

Library of Congress Cataloging-in-Publication Data can be found at www.loc.gov.

Printed in the United States of America

25 24 23 22 21 20 19
7   6   5   4   3

To Sandy,
the most wonderful person
in the world

Contents

INTRODUCTION: Opposites Attract . . . and Drive You Nutty! *xi*

PART ONE: **We Can't Talk!**
1. The War between the Sexes *3*
2. Mr. Control Meets Mrs. Closeness *11*
3. Why Your Conversations Don't Go Anywhere *19*

PART TWO: **We Need Communication Skills!**
4. Women, Drop Your Crowbars! *29*
5. Men, You Gotta Listen! *37*
6. Make Time to Talk *45*
7. To Kill a Pattern, Interrupt It *53*
8. Women, Use One-Way Communication *63*
9. Women, Praise and Praise and Praise Him *71*
10. Men, Open Up Your Clams! *77*
11. A Clam's Top Nine Conversation Starters *85*

PART THREE: **We Need to Build Deeper Conversations Every Week!**
12. "What's the Matter with Your Brain?" *97*
13. Connect Your Brains with the "Train" *105*
14. A Great Talk Takes a Week *113*

PART FOUR: **We Need to Talk about Difficult Topics!**
15. He Doesn't Want to Talk about Difficult Topics *123*
16. How to Talk about Difficult Topics *129*

PART FIVE: We Need to Spiritually Bond!

17. You Want the Gold, Don't You? *139*

18. It's All about Jesus *147*

19. Praying as a Couple *155*

20. Spiritual Conversations as a Couple *163*

21. Reading the Bible as a Couple *173*

22. "But My Partner Can't or Won't
    Spiritually Bond" *183*

23. The Adventure Begins *197*

Additional Resources *201*
About the Authors *203*

Introduction

Opposites Attract . . . and Drive You Nutty!

IF YOU COME TO A DR. DAVID CLARKE, Men Are Clams, Women Are Crowbars Seminar, you will hear me start by saying:

"Women. Will men ever really understand women? The answer, of course, is *no*. I mean, who are we kidding? This concludes my seminar. Thank you for coming."

As I begin to walk off the stage, there is nervous laughter in the audience. The couples are thinking, *Is he serious? Is the seminar over?*

Then I return to center stage and launch into my explanation of how difficult it is for a man to understand a woman. Here's how it goes.

"Women. Will men ever really understand women? Did you ever notice that most women have a lot of clothes? Dresses, skirts, pants, blouses. And don't forget the accessories: shoes, belts, scarves, things for their hair. The list is endless! Most women have more clothes right now than they could ever possibly wear in one lifetime. But they keep buying more! Why? We don't know.

"Take a look at the closet shared by the average couple. Three-quarters of that baby is jammed full of the woman's clothes. If the light is just right, and you look really close, you can just barely make out the tiny, cramped section the man is forced to use.

"It's not fair! It's not right! And it needs to stop. Ladies, we've had enough. The party's over. I'm starting a new national organization for men. I call it 'Take Back the Closet.'

"Speaking of clothes, there is a situation that has puzzled men for centuries. Here is a woman who owns enough clothes and accessories to outfit a small European country. She stands in front of her closet—and I mean *her* closet—and in all sincerity, says these classic words, 'I just don't have a thing to wear.' What? You've got to be kidding! The correct statement, my dear, is, 'Out of the thousands of choices I have, I can't decide what to wear.'

"Another quality about women that men don't understand is the way they talk. Women love details, and they can remember with astonishing clarity every event of their day—in fact, every event of the past twenty-five years.

"This is fine in and of itself. The problem is that a woman wants to share all the details with her man. The man wants the big picture, the overall sketch. He gets drowned in too many details while the woman spends twenty minutes describing what happened, how she feels about it, and how it affected her life. And that's just to cover the time from her car door to the mall entrance. She's just getting started!

"For me, as a man, listening to this kind of story is like ordering a pepperoni pizza and having it delivered one pepperoni at a time. Please give me the whole pizza—give it to me now! Get to the point before I die of old age.

"We men have also never really understood why women cry and cry so much. Women cry when they're happy. They cry when they're sad. They cry when they're angry. They cry when they're tired. Sometimes they cry and don't even know why. Now, that's spooky.

"There is no more pitiful sight in the world than a man whose woman is crying. He doesn't know what to do. Everything he tries seems to backfire and lead to more crying, which is the last thing he wants. If he moves in close and tries to comfort her, she says, 'Back off, bud. How dare you touch me! You caused this problem.' If he backs off and gives some space to the woman he loves, she says, 'That's right, ignore me. You never cared.'"

I look at the audience and say with a straight face, "Look, I'm living with a woman. Help me!" And then I say, "Men, can I get an *amen*?"

All the men give me a huge amen because they can relate to what I'm saying. The men know it's all true, and now a relationship expert is actually saying it out loud. Plus, they realize with great relief that I'm not going to bash men in my seminar.

But why should the men have all the fun? At this point, I turn my attention to describing men. Fair is fair, and the men must take their turn in the hot seat. Here's how this seminar segment goes.

"Well, enough about women. I've been married since 1982 to Sandy, and I have a lot of material from my experience with the opposite sex. But it's time to get to the men.

"Men. Will women ever really understand men? During courtship, the man is the absolute spirit of romance. He's a cross between George Clooney and Brad Pitt: suave, charming, attentive, and caring. His only goal in life is to please his woman. Her every wish is his command. But what happens after marriage? A terrible transformation takes place that his wife can't understand.

"After the wedding and a few years into the marriage, things are just a little bit different. The man becomes the absolute spirit of selfishness. He's about as romantic as a wet blanket. His idea of a romantic evening is eating a big, juicy steak (that the woman cooks), renting a war movie, and falling asleep on the couch with his hand in the potato chip bag. The poor woman goes from the days of wine and roses to the days of cheeseburgers and dirty underwear. It's a long drop!

"Another nasty surprise for women is learning that men don't like to do routine household chores. Men consider laundry, washing the dishes, and vacuuming beneath their dignity and position. Men prefer big, glamorous projects like building the Panama Canal, buying a new car, remodeling the den, or installing a sprinkler system. These are jobs that will be noticed and stand the test of time.

"Ladies, isn't it amazing how a man who holds a responsible job requiring hard work and a variety of skills can be so lazy and useless at home? When a man comes through the front door, his IQ drops forty points, and he is suddenly unable to operate appliances and perform simple housecleaning tasks. And when the man does complete a small household chore, what does he immediately expect? You know, ladies. A parade in his honor and the Nobel Peace Prize! If the woman doesn't sink to her knees and thankfully kiss his ring, he pouts. He did a job, and no one noticed. Poor thing!

"The real capper for women is their frustrated attempts to engage men in deep, personal conversations. Men aren't very good at deep, personal conversations. It seems to women that all men think about is food, their jobs, sports, and sex—not necessarily in that order. Men don't talk much, and when they do open their mouths it's to belch or ask you to pass the mustard.

"A woman watches a man express a broad range of intense emotions during a ball game on television: rage, joy, fear, passion. I mean, he's all over the map emotionally. After the game, she asks him how his day was, and he says, 'Okay.' And the crazy thing is, he expects that one word to satisfy her curiosity. 'Oh! It was okay. Thanks for sharing. That tells me so much.'

"After years of clinical experience and careful research, I have discovered that most men have a very limited vocabulary after marriage. In fact, the vast majority of married men utter only four phrases: 'I don't know.' 'Did you say something, dear?' 'I need a shirt for tomorrow.' And, of course, the most important question, 'What's for dinner?'"

As I conclude my description of men, I ask the women, "Isn't it incredibly difficult to live with a man? Can I get an *amen*?" Of course, the ladies give an even louder amen than the men. When the volume dies down, I fake minor irritability and say to these women, "Well, you don't have to shout it!"

Dave Clarke Gets It

At this early point in the seminar, the couples know I get it. I understand the incredible differences between men and women. I should get it— I've been married to my beautiful blonde, Sandy, for more than thirty years. I've also been working with couples in therapy for thirty years as a clinical psychologist.

William Clarke Gets It Too

William Clarke, my writing partner, has been married to my mom, Kathleen, for sixty years. He's a master's-level marriage and family therapist who has been working with couples for more than thirty years.

My marriage, my experience as a marital therapist, my dad's wisdom, and the teaching in the Bible have all helped me discover principles that help couples understand their outrageous differences and create real closeness.

Some of you may be saying: "Dave, you're dealing in stereotypes. The actions and roles you have described don't apply to all men and women." My response is: "My descriptions of men and women in this book don't always apply, but in my personal and professional experience, they often apply."

Crazy or Close?

These differences can be funny. Even entertaining. But if you don't find ways to deal successfully with them, they will do great damage to your relationship.

Your male-female differences will take you as a couple down one of two paths. If you take the most popular, well-traveled path, your differences will drive you crazy and ruin your relationship.

I wrote this book to take you down the hard-to-find, lightly traveled path. On this path, you learn how to work with your differences to achieve crazy-good intimacy. This is the path you want to be on and God wants you to be on.

I'm going to show the two of you exactly how to find this path and stay on it—for a lifetime.

Who Will Benefit from This Book?

If you are in a serious romantic relationship, this book is for you. It is designed for couples who are married *and* couples who are not married. My principles can help every couple dramatically deepen their level of intimacy.

Though I'm writing to married couples, if you're not married, this book can give you the confidence to marry and the tools to stay happily married.

When the Roles Are Reversed

The main theme of my approach is the Clam-Crowbar difference. When I say men are Clams, I mean they clam up and do not share personally, do not share *themselves*. When I say women are Crowbars, I mean they work too hard to try to open up their Clams, their men.

In 25 percent of couples, these roles are reversed: The woman is the Clam and the man is the Crowbar. Not to worry. This is completely normal. My principles still apply.

The Path to a Crazy Good Relationship

Here's where I'm going to take you. I'll teach you how to work with your Clam-Crowbar differences to master three vital relationship skills:

- emotional intimacy through deeper communication
- the ability to talk about any topic, including difficult topics
- intimacy with God as a couple through spiritual bonding

I've divided the book into five sections:

1. We Can't Talk!
2. We Need Communication Skills!
3. We Need to Build Deeper Conversations Every Week!
4. We Need to Talk about Difficult Topics!
5. We Need to Spiritually Bond!

Are you ready to take your relationship to the next level? The best level? Let's get started.

ASK YOURSELVES THESE QUESTIONS

1. What differences attracted you to your partner?

2. To which of the differences in this chapter do you relate the most?

3. Which of your differences are funny and are not an issue? Which differences have the potential to cause real problems in your relationship?

4. Do you want to learn to use your differences to build a great relationship? What would keep you from reading through this book and applying my strategies?

PART ONE

We Can't Talk!

CHAPTER I

THE WAR BETWEEN
THE SEXES

THE FIRST THREE MONTHS OF the Dave and Sandy Clarke marriage was brutally tough. All of our differences hit the fan and we struggled to adjust. Battling the huge rats in our nasty little apartment turned out to be the easy part. Battling each other was the big problem!

One of our major differences was in the area of chores. I had very few chores to do in my childhood. My mom did most of the work in the home and seemed very happy to do these jobs.

Sandy, on the other hand, did a ton of chores as she grew up in the Martin household. I think her parents may have broken a number of child labor laws. She had chores in the morning, chores after school, and chores in the evening. Compared to my home, hers was a prison chain gang.

Our marriage began with Sandy doing pretty much everything in our home: cleaning, laundry, dishes, cooking, grocery shopping . . . I even had her type—late at night—my papers for my seminary classes. Oh, and she also had a full-time job outside the home.

I figured Sandy, like my mom, would love doing all these things for me. She didn't. She really, really didn't. A few months into our marriage, she sat me down and told me it was time I grew up and saved her from death by exhaustion.

I'm happy to report I did step up and took over the laundry and the dishes. And I did my own typing. The problem was, this was just one area where we had to work at our differences!

Marriage Is a Terrible Idea!

The one problem with marriage is that a man and a woman have to live together. Without question, this is the worst idea anyone ever came up with. It's not just a bad idea. It's a ridiculously bad idea!

It's like putting a deer into the tiger's cage at the zoo and hoping the two of them can get along. I don't think so. There's going to be trouble. And it won't take long.

The only thing more difficult than living with a member of the opposite sex is . . . actually, there is nothing more difficult.

I had a dream that a group of the world's greatest scientists, the most brilliant minds of our generation, came together at a retreat in the Swiss Alps (important retreats are always held in the Swiss Alps). They met to answer this most important question: "What is the quickest and most effective way to drive a person insane?"

The learned men and women went into a conference room to deliberate. Five minutes later they emerged with a one-word answer: "Marriage."

We don't need a group of distinguished scientists to tell us what we already know, do we? If you're married, you know what I'm talking about.

Is there anything more frustrating, nerve-racking, and just plain exasperating than living with the opposite sex?

Marriage Changes Everything

Dating is fantastic. Courtship is bliss. Engagement is super. You notice some differences between you, but they are small, trivial, even petty. They're cute. You even laugh about them.

But when you marry and move in together, within two years your differences become big, dramatic, and incredibly annoying. You are well past the trivial and cute phase. No one is laughing anymore. Your home is filled with moaning, sighing, and the grinding of two sets of teeth.

In addition to your basic male-female differences, now you will be forced to deal with a variety of personality differences. You'll be convinced that your spouse is trying to drive you crazy.

How could you have ended up with someone who turned out to be such a nuisance? You'd like to walk up to your partner's parents and say, "Thanks for raising the world's biggest pest!"

Check out this catalog of personality and lifestyle differences. I know you will recognize yourself and your spouse in some of these.

The Thermostat Wars

One spouse is always hot. One is always cold. Complaining about the temperature and sneaking to change the thermostat becomes commonplace. You wake up in the middle of the night freezing, or you wake up dying of the heat. And you know your spouse has made a successful commando run to the thermostat.

Night Owl and Morning Glory

Morning Glory wakes up singing at 5:00 a.m. without an alarm, but is brain-dead by 9:00 p.m.

Night Owl comes alive at 9:00 p.m. and is ready to party, but has to be hit with a cattle prod to get up in the morning. When you are alive and energized, it's fun to deal with someone in a catatonic state.

Mr. Crude and Mrs. Manners

Mr. Crude belches, even passes gas on a regular basis. He sees this as being "manly." It's also being manly not to feel too bad about it and rarely say, "Excuse me" after the offensive behavior.

Mrs. Manners is horrified and offended by his complete lack of taste. (In some cultures, belching after a meal is an expected and cherished act. Women in those cultures are thrilled by it. The moral: Marry into one of those cultures if you want to keep barking out those belches.)

Pack Rat and Garage Saler

The Pack Rat keeps everything, including every school paper the children bring home. The Pack Rat hogs every square inch of storage room to hoard the treasure trove of trivialities and minutia.

The Garage Saler feels buried alive under a mountain of useless stuff and wants to sell everything.

The Slob and the Neatnik

One spouse is a rumpled, crumpled, and disorganized mess maker. This spouse never puts anything away and sees no reason to clean when the place is just going to get dirty again.

The opposite of this is the Neatnik, who wants to live in a museum of order and cleanliness. Messiness is seen as evidence of a weak, disturbed mind.

The Slob says, "Why make the bed when we're just going to mess it up again?" Sadly, the Slob is deadly serious. The Neatnik replies, "I'll tell you why. Because we're civilized human beings, not animals."

Ratty Clothes Man

This husband parades around in twenty-year-old, threadbare T-shirts, college sweatshirts, and gym shorts from his high school days. His old clothes are filled with holes and hideous stains, but he considers them old friends. He's horribly out of fashion. But he's comfortable.

The wife can barely handle his nasty, disreputable, shameful clothes inside their home. Her greatest fear is that he will go out in public wearing his disgusting rags.

Social Media Maven

She spends hours a day doing Facebook, Twitter, Instagram, Pinterest, and every other existing social-media channel. Her every meal, her every shopping trip, her every day at work, her every experience, and her every thought must be shared with her massive network of very close "friends."

Sports Man

To say that he is into sports would be the understatement of the century. He lives for sports, and every game, every event is of vital importance. He watches games on television and listens on the radio, and he checks the progress of games and the statistics on his iPhone or iPad or computer.

He's in at least three fantasy leagues at the same time. He's on the verge of quitting his job so he can have time to keep up with his players and their production.

HGN and Hallmark Channel Diva

She watches only two television channels, and they are every man's living nightmare. On HGN, she watches wealthy couples redecorate, remodel, and buy fantastically expensive homes. The really bad news is, these shows give her all kinds of makeover ideas for her home. Expensive ideas.

Most men would rather—if they could afford it—remodel the home or buy a new one rather than watch the *other* channel preferred by the woman. Imagine every sappy, insipid, predictable, silly, romantic movie collected in one place. Oh, that's right. You don't have to imagine it. Press three numbers on the remote and there it is. It is called the Hallmark Channel.

As he watches yet another small-town girl fall in love with a big-city guy who has a mean fiancée, this husband thinks, *I am being punished. And I must have been awful.*

Never on Time
One spouse is chronically late for everything. Church. Social events. School activities. Doctors' appointments. Work. Airline flights. He or she is usually married to someone who wants to be fifteen minutes early for everything. They make a tough combination.

I'm Going to Die—Again
This partner thinks that every illness or pain is a symptom of a final, fatal disease. Pain in the chest means catastrophic heart problems. Pain in the back means the kidneys are failing. Pain in the rear (he or she has become a pain in the rear to the spouse) means rectal cancer. And so on.

I could go on and on. There are sunny optimists married to gloom-and-doom pessimists. Bedroom television watchers who have the set on to help them go to sleep. Physical fitness enthusiasts who pressure their spouses to work out and consume fruit drinks. Vegetarians. Lip-smacking, slurping soup eaters. Snorers. Bed hogs. Toss and turners. Putterers. Social butterflies. Lone Rangers. Free spenders. Fort Knox savers. Reckless drivers. The rare drivers who drive the speed limit.

The Biggest and Most Destructive Difference of All
Every married person must put up with a variety of their spouse's annoying differences and habits. Some can even be amusing. The ability to laugh at ourselves helps to lessen the tension. What's *not* funny is that many of these differences push us further apart.

Why do our differences push us further away from one another? Because we do not learn how to manage them, how to adjust to them.

And we don't learn how because of the biggest and most destructive difference between men and women: how we communicate.

Because we aren't communicating successfully, we can't understand and deal effectively with our male-female differences. So we experience a gradual breakdown in intimacy. Fewer and fewer needs are met in the relationship. Our emotional, spiritual, and physical bonds are diminished. It doesn't happen right away, but it happens.

I cannot overstate the importance of healthy communication in a marriage. Without it, you will lose all your intimacy. With it, you will develop a deep and lasting intimacy.

Because men are Clams and women are Crowbars, we start every interaction—and I mean every interaction—miles away from an emotional connection. First, we need to figure out how to get past the Clam-Crowbar blocks to break through to real communication.

I'm going to help you do that. Starting right now.

ASK YOURSELVES THESE QUESTIONS

1. Which of these personality and lifestyle differences I've described ring a bell with you?

2. If I haven't covered some key differences in your relationship, talk to each other about these differences now.

3. Which of your differences are not a big deal, and which are really more than annoying and are causing problems?

4. How intimate is your relationship right now (1 being very low and 10 being high in intimacy)? What differences are stopping you from getting more intimate?

MR. CONTROL MEETS
MRS. CLOSENESS

USE YOUR IMAGINATION, AND picture this scenario. I'll bet you'll recognize it. We have two persons in a relationship: Bob and Betty. Near the end of one day, Betty is attempting to develop a conversation with Bob. You see, Betty wants to learn more about Bob, to get him to share some personal information. And so she asks him some questions.

"How was your day?"

"What are you thinking about right now?"

"How do you feel?"

Women have been asking their men these questions for centuries. Women love to ask these questions. What they don't realize is it drives their men crazy.

Betty is probing, trying to get inside the man she loves. She wants to know Bob better. She wants to reach him on a deeper level. Good luck, Betty!

To Betty's dismay and growing irritation, Bob does not present any personal information. He becomes defensive and acts as though he's being tortured by the secret police. He's holding Betty at arm's length and won't talk personally. Unknown to her, he feels she is invading his private self.

In response to Betty's questions, Bob grunts a few times (we men are good at this), makes some vague statements, and falls silent. He is not going to talk!

Betty isn't satisfied with this reaction at all. She wants more than grunts in her marriage! She wants talking, dialogue (that's a conversation involving at least *two* people), sharing, and closeness. Betty presses for some response. Bob finally gets angry, snaps at her verbally, and leaves the room. Both Bob and Betty end up angry, hurt, and confused. Betty feels unfulfilled and unloved.

A Classic Male-Female Conversation

This scenario is not new for Bob and Betty. It has happened many times before, and unless they learn what's causing it, it will continue to happen. And each time it happens, they've lost another opportunity for intimacy.

This is a classic male-female interaction, isn't it? The woman asks questions and tries desperately to get the man to open up. She's the Crowbar. The man resists her attempts and does not open up. He shuts down. He pulls in. He's the Clam.

Does this Clam-Crowbar interaction sound familiar? I know it does. This happened to Sandy and me a million times in the first ten years of our marriage. She'd ask me these same questions, and I would immediately shut down and give her nothing.

Sandy would get very frustrated, and I would get very defensive and irritated. Not good. We still loved each other, but our conversations were going nowhere.

Finally, we figured out what was going wrong. With God's help, we took steps to repair it. So can you two.

Keep in mind that in this Clam-Crowbar scenario, there is no good guy and bad guy. Neither person is acting maliciously or with the intent to hurt the other. What's happening is two persons operating on completely different levels, these levels unknown to the other.

Why Are We So Different?

Why are women Crowbars? Why do they pry and prod and probe for personal information from their men? All you men are thinking, *Yeah. Why do they do that?* I'll tell you why.

In a relationship, women want closeness—not just physical closeness, but emotional, intellectual, spiritual closeness. That's their number one priority. For them, if they have no closeness in a relationship, they have nothing. They literally can't be happy and satisfied.

Why are men Clams? Why do they shut down and deny the women that they love what they want and *need*? All you women are thinking, *Tell me, please. I've always wondered why.* I'll tell you.

In a relationship, men want control, which is directly connected to their view of themselves, their self-esteem. That's their number one priority. It is an essential masculine trait. For them, if they have no control in a relationship, they have nothing.

Men and women operate on these different levels, closeness and control, because of two main reasons. One, it is simply genetic. We're born to function in these two ways. Two—and this is the real clincher—we're actually taught to behave in these ways throughout our upbringing.

What Makes a Clam a Clam

We men are taught from birth to develop these personal qualities in our relationships: respect, status, strength, power, and independence. These are all qualities designed to give us a sense of control.

Do you ever watch little boys when they play? For years, I watched our son, Will, play with his buddies. It's a violent, competitive, dog-eat-dog jungle. Who won, who got the most points, who killed the most enemies, who scored the winning points? It's a battle to see who is the strongest, the fastest, the best. There is very little talking. Only grunts, car noises, and yelling short words.

And what little boy hasn't been told, "Men don't cry"? Crying is weakness. Don't express your true feelings and thoughts. That will give your opponent the edge. Gotta be cool under pressure; gotta be calm in a crisis; gotta be in control. That's being a man. This message is drilled into us men and we learn it well.

Our cultural heroes are men of action, drive, and impressive accomplishment. We love movie characters who overcome impossible odds to kill the bad guys, rescue the girl, and save the world.

We love sports stars who make the last-second touchdown to win the game, who get the hit in the bottom of the ninth to drive in the winning run, and who hammer in the thunderous dunk that shatters the backboard.

We love the billionaire businessman who amasses great wealth, achieves far-reaching power, and has all the fun toys.

These male heroes are tough, determined customers who man up when the chips are down and get the job done. They are not sensitive, touchy-feely types known for being in touch with their emotions. And they rarely have long-term, close relationships with women. Usually, our heroes have a series of short-term relationships with women. If they get married, they don't stay married for long.

What Makes a Crowbar a Crowbar

Women are taught from birth to develop these personal qualities in relationships: connection, cooperation, openness, understanding, and intimacy. Wow! What a difference! These are all qualities that are designed to produce *closeness*.

When little girls play, it's a more peaceful and cooperative environment. I ought to know. I have three daughters. They don't try to kill each other or fight to prove who's the best. They work together. They consider how others think and feel. There's *a lot of talking*, and the talking is all focused on getting to know each other. The play of little girls is relationship-oriented, and the relationships they build are all-important to them.

Let me illustrate with how my three girls played Barbie dolls with me back in the day. They are all adults now, but these Barbie playtimes are crystal clear in my mind. Let's just say we played Barbies a lot.

They lead me to the clubhouse, a big room in our home where all the toys are kept. I'm faced with a big pile of forty-five naked Barbie dolls. It's a little overwhelming. The first thing we each have to do is select one Barbie that each of us will be. When each of us chooses a Barbie, we become that Barbie for the duration of the game. We will talk and act through that Barbie. ("I am Barbie.")

Since they are naked, we have to dress our Barbies. Ever dressed a Barbie? You'd think it would be a snap since Barbie is unbelievably skinny. Guess again. Barbie is extremely thin, but her clothes are even thinner. It takes twenty minutes just to tug on a top and a pair of pants!

And when the last Barbie is finally dressed, the rule is: Every Barbie has to feel good about every other Barbie's outfit. If even one of the other Barbies doesn't think I look good in my outfit, my Barbie has to change clothes. "Oh, Barbie! Those green shorts just don't go with that pink top." My Barbie tries to argue, but inevitably she is outvoted, and I put on my Barbie what her Barbie friends feel looks best on her.

Finally, all the Barbies are dressed and happy and full of self-esteem. Now comes the real challenge—at least for me. The Barbies have to decide where to go in their nice clothes. Again, all the Barbies have to feel good about the decision that is made, or it doesn't happen. Each Barbie mentions where she would like to go, and then the entire group discusses the idea. Unless all the Barbies agree, they go nowhere.

My Barbie says, "Let's go to the beach." Barbie Number Two says, "Yes." Barbie Number Three says, "Yes." Barbie Number Four says, "No. I don't want to. I might get sunburned." So the deal is off.

Undaunted, my Barbie tosses her head back, stretches both her bony arms out, and says, "It's three votes to one. We're going to the beach. If you don't want to come, tough! Stay here."

Oh, no! That's not how sensitive, relationship-oriented little girls operate. Instead, the other Barbies say to my Barbie, "No. Just *one* of us can't go. We all have to agree, or we can't go. You know that."

In all the years I've played Barbies, we've never actually gone anywhere.

Emily, Leeann, and Nancy would rather sit around on the floor of the clubhouse and talk about where to go than go somewhere and have even one Barbie not feel good about it. My point? That's women.

And let's not forget: For girls, it's okay to cry. In fact, it's important and expected to open up and tell secrets, because this will lead to closeness. And closeness is what little girls want.

We Can't Talk!

Eventually, little boys and girls grow up, but how they operate in relationships stays exactly the same as it has always been. So when men and women come together in conversation, there isn't just the potential for trouble. Oh, no! There is an absolute *guarantee* of trouble!

Here we have adult Bob, who has a built-in alarm system to warn him of incoming threats to his control. And Betty, the guided missile, who's going to get close if it's the last thing she does. It's not a good combination. In fact, it's a disaster waiting to happen.

Let's take a look at what is happening inside the man and the woman during a classic attempt at a deeper, closeness-creating conversation.

ASK YOURSELVES THESE QUESTIONS

1. Can you relate to the classic male-female conversation I discussed, and the typical outcome? How many times has this happened to you?

2. Think of a recent example in which you felt the Clam-Crowbar scenario at work in your marriage. Sir, tell your woman how you felt when she pressed you for conversation. Ma'am, tell your man how you felt when he clammed up on you.

3. Sir, talk about how you learned to stay in control as you grew up. Who are your heroes, and how do they express their need for control in their lives? How important to you is staying in control in your relationship with your partner?

4. Ma'am, talk about how you learned to value and pursue closeness as you grew up. Talk about Barbies and other activities in which closeness was important. How important to you is experiencing closeness in your relationship?

CHAPTER 3

WHY YOUR CONVERSATIONS DON'T GO ANYWHERE

THE TWO OF YOU ARE IN YOUR CAR and about to hop on the highway. Your plan is to drive to a fun destination and have a wonderful day together. It's only you two, because you've just dumped—I mean dropped off—your children with the grandparents or the sitter.

As you get on the interstate and begin to accelerate, your anticipation and excitement turn to frustration and nausea. Up ahead there is a sea of red brake lights. It's a massive traffic jam, and all the lanes are blocked. You brake to a halt and sit there.

It wouldn't be so bad if you at least were moving. No such luck. You are completely stopped. You're not moving an inch. You're not going anywhere.

Conversational Gridlock

I've just described most, if not all, of your attempts at intimate conversation, haven't I? Just like you in your car in a traffic jam, your conversations get stuck and don't go anywhere. There's no movement. You can't make any progress.

You need to find a way around the gridlock.

I know the way. For the past thirty years, it's been my ministry and my living to help couples develop consistently deep, intimate conversations.

To break out of conversational gridlock, it's important to know what's going on inside yourself and your partner as you try to connect on an emotional level.

What's Happening inside Bob?

What is Bob the Clam really thinking and feeling as his partner asks him to talk to her?

When Betty asks Bob to open up and share what's inside, his alarm goes off. He automatically responds with defensive maneuvers. He doesn't even know why he's doing it! His responses are unconscious reflexes. It's what he's always done in this situation.

Deep down, Bob believes that sharing secrets about his inner thoughts and feelings will make him vulnerable and cause him to seem weak. With another man, in the business world, it would. But not with his woman. Not with his precious, lifelong lover!

Bob doesn't reveal his personal thoughts and feelings to anyone. He's a man, and so by nature he keeps everything personal in the vault. That way, no one can do him any harm.

Also, Bob has never—and I mean never—seen another significant man in his life ever open up and share something personal. Dad didn't do it. Stepdad didn't do it. Neither grandpa did. Uncles and cousins didn't do it. No coach, teacher, or boss did it.

If Dad—the most important man in his life—ever did share himself personally with Mom, it was behind closed doors. But what Bob did see a million times was his dad stiffening up and resisting Mom's attempts at conversation. So Bob learned from his dad that you keep your guard up with a woman. That's what a man does.

As crazy and ridiculous as it seems, Bob thinks if he opens up to

Betty, he risks getting hurt and being dominated. Most of all, he thinks he risks losing control.

He will not take the chance that these bad things will happen.

"My Bad Day Is My Secret"

Let's see Bob the Clam in action. After a bad day at work, a man will get home and make a beeline for his wife. He'll hug her, pull back, and say, "Honey, I had a bad day and need to pour out my heart to you. Let's find a private place to talk right now."

Is this what Bob does and what almost all men do? Are you kidding? Never! He won't appear out of control, or weak, or vulnerable.

When his woman asks Bob how his day was, he'll pick one of several stock replies. It's amazing that she continues to ask, day after day, since she always gets the same responses. He'll say, "Fine." Fine? What does "fine" mean? Or he'll say, "Okay." Hey, that tells her a lot. Or he'll go with, "Not bad." Well, that narrows it down; at least she can rule out bad.

All these answers are safe responses that tell his woman nothing and keep him in control. Every man is a master at sidestepping questions and holding back on information and feelings the woman needs. That's right, I said *needs*.

"What's Wrong, Honey?"

The woman knows her man is upset about something. He's tense and quieter than usual. Her intuition is right on—for all the good it'll do her. Her chances of finding out what's on his mind are just about dead zero. She has a better chance at winning the lottery or being the first woman on Mars. (Actually, if the man never opens up, she'll want to be the first woman on Mars.)

Nevertheless, hope springs eternal, and she'll ask him a question when she already knows the answer: "Is there anything bothering you?" He replies with a straight face, "No." Liar. She tries again, being more direct. "What's wrong, honey?" He answers, again with a straight face, "Nothing." Big, fat liar.

If the man provides any information at all, it is precious little, and it is intended to get the woman off his back. At the most, he'll say, "Okay. I had a bad day. But . . . I don't want to talk about it." Big, fat cop-out.

Bob believes that talking about his bad day with his wife will make him feel worse and make his stress level go up. He's wrong, but he's conditioned to believe this. He will not discuss what happened today and his painful emotions. He will stuff it and move on.

"I'm Not Good at Personal Sharing"

Bob also fears that he won't do well if he shares personally. Most men are very competitive. He knows Betty is much better at this personal sharing stuff, and if he can't win or at least do well, he won't try.

It's an old lesson we men are taught as we grow up: Never, ever let a woman beat you at anything. It's a stupid lesson, but it's taught to us by male friends and older male role models, and we learn it.

Four Classic Male Responses

Because of Bob's incorrect beliefs and intense drive to *remain in control*, he does one of four things in response to Betty's attempts to open him up.

1. Bob gives a safe response that tells the woman nothing.
2. Bob remains silent.
3. Bob gets angry and snaps verbally at Betty.
4. Bob physically leaves the situation.

Of course, Bob may make all four responses in a row. Whatever his response, conversational gridlock occurs. The conversation—which barely started—is officially over.

What Is Happening inside Betty?

What is Betty, the Crowbar, thinking and feeling as she tries unsuccessfully to pry open the Clam?

Betty watches Bob go into his Clam routine and works her crowbar harder and faster. She escalates. She gets more intense because she sees her opportunity for closeness slipping away.

Betty thinks, and may actually verbalize, "Talk to me! I want to help. I want to know you. I want to share life with you. I want to be your soul mate. Stop avoiding me."

She may say—as one client of mine did to her husband, "If I wanted company without conversation, I'd live with a dog, or a cat, or a goldfish!"

"Let Me Tell You about My Bad Day"

When a woman has a bad day, she can't wait to talk about it—with her man, her mother, a sister, some close friends, even the woman she just met in the grocery store line. She always feels better after expressing herself.

So naturally, if her man has had a bad day, the woman cannot understand his refusal to talk about it. She'll say to him, "Honey, it'll help to talk about it. You'll get it off your chest, and you won't be as stressed. That's what I'm here for—to talk to when life is hard."

It blows her mind that he chooses, again and again, to hold in his stress and hurt himself. Does he enjoy pain and suffering?

"I Need to Know"

The woman is also naturally curious and is dying to know what happened to her man today. If his day was a good day, she wants to know why it was good. If it was a bad day, she wants to know why it was bad. She lives in a world of details and can't ever get enough of them. Incredibly, she can hold all these details in her head at one time.

Women want to know everything that's going on in the lives of their loved ones. The smallest event, the most trivial tidbit, is of interest to her and collected. She then uses all these details to assist her in her nurturing role.

"I Can Help You"

If she learns what's happened to her husband, she believes she can help him. And . . . she's right! Maybe she can say something to help. Maybe she can do something to help. Maybe she can touch him, support him, and encourage him. Maybe she can pray for him.

When the man she loves won't talk about his troubles with her, all these maybes end up as a little pile of conversational sawdust on the floor. These potentially helpful, intimate conversations go nowhere.

She knows he's upset. She can feel his pain. She wants desperately to find out what has gone wrong for him so she can nurture him. If he won't tell her—and he won't—there's nothing she can do.

She is not only frustrated, she is hurt. She feels rejected because she thinks her man doesn't trust her enough to open up to her.

"I'm Gonna Get That Clam to Open"

When Betty hits gridlock in a conversation, she doesn't give up easily. When he won't talk about his bad day, or just plain won't talk personally about his day, Betty thinks, *If I just push hard enough, I'll break through and get that Clam open.*

Wrong. Dead wrong. This approach will make him clam up even tighter.

I have gone back to the days of cavemen and dinosaurs in my research of male-female conversation. I've scoured libraries, searched using Google, pored over historical records of all civilizations, and talked to a lot of really old people. I even asked Siri.

There is no recorded incident of a man breaking down and sharing any personal information under his woman's questioning.

Sorry, all you Bettys, your man will not be the first.

"Does He Care about Me?"

When Bob clams up, Betty also thinks, *Bob knows I want closeness, and he is deliberately denying it to me.* It's a small jump to her next few thoughts: *He doesn't care about me. I wonder if he truly loves me.*

All you Bettys: Listen to me. I understand this thinking and your pain. I've heard you through hundreds of other women. But you're wrong. Unless you're with a narcissist or a sociopath, your man is not intentionally and maliciously holding back closeness from you.

He does care about you. He does love you. He just doesn't know how to love you in the way you need to be loved. Not yet.

What's happening when he clams up and will not let you inside is that he feels his control is being threatened, and he can't let that happen. Just as you don't mean to threaten his control, he doesn't mean to hurt you with his Clam response.

It's time for me to show you exactly how to get around your Clam-Crowbar gridlock and into conversational closeness.

ASK YOURSELVES THESE QUESTIONS

1. Sir, who were the important men in your life who modeled how to not open up and share your personal feelings?

2. Sir, why don't you tell her what you are thinking and feeling when she asks you for personal information?

3. Which of the four classic male responses do you use most? Why?

4. Ma'am, who were the important women in your life who taught you how to use a crowbar to try to get a man to open up?

5. Ma'am, tell your man why it is so important to you that he tell you about his day . . . whether it was good or bad.

6. Tell him—honestly—how much it hurts you when he will not share with you his personal thoughts and feelings about his day, about you, and about your relationship.

PART TWO

We Need Communication Skills!

CHAPTER 4

WOMEN, DROP YOUR CROWBARS!

HERE'S A DIALOGUE I'VE HAD WITH hundreds and hundreds of women in my therapy office:

> **Woman:** Dr. Clarke, my husband won't open up and talk to me.

> **Me:** I know.

> **Woman:** He'll talk with me only about superficial, trivial things like sports, home repair projects, and politics.

> **Me:** I know.

> **Woman:** He refuses to share his personal thoughts and feelings.

> **Me:** I know.

Woman: I married him because I love him, and because of that, I want to get to know him and everything about him: how he sees the world and himself, his relationship with God, his relationship with me, what makes him happy, what stresses him, his hopes for the future.

Me: I know.

Woman: Why won't he open up and talk personally with me?

Me: I'm looking at the reason.

Woman: What do you mean? You're saying I'm the reason he doesn't talk on a deeper level?

Me: Yes, that is what I'm saying. His pattern of not talking personally is partly his fault. But it's also partly your fault.

When I tell a woman that she is part of the problem in the communication area, she typically doesn't take it well. She gets angry. She gets offended. She gets huffy.

It's Easy to Blame the Guy

Look, it's very easy to blame the man for the lack of intimate conversation in the relationship. His mistakes are obvious. He won't allow closeness and resists the woman's attempts to achieve emotional intimacy. He won't talk about his life. He won't talk about his work, especially if he is unhappy about it. He won't talk about what's bothering him. He won't talk about his relationship with his woman. He won't. He won't. He won't.

It's true. He won't.

Men have their faults, and I'm hard on men in my therapy office and in my marriage seminars. Men are half the problem in the communication arena. Guess who is the other half?

Women Are Half the Problem

That's right. For every Clam there is a Crowbar. I'm pretty hard on women, too. Why? Because women feed into communication issues just as much as their men do.

Ladies, there's one thing you are doing in conversation—over and over and over—that is preventing the very intimacy you so desperately want and need. This mistake is part of the reason your man clams up.

I've already brought up this mistake, but I want to drill down and make it crystal clear. Because when you correct this mistake, there is a good chance your Clam will open up to you.

Stop Trying So Hard

Many of you Crowbars make the mistake of escalating, getting too intense in your efforts to open up your Clam. You are determined to get into that Clam.

You know—and you are right—that if the Clam stays shut, your relationship will wither and die. There will be no closeness. You will live separate lives. If you stay together, it will be a cold and lonely existence.

So to prevent this disaster, you beat on that Clam and beat on that Clam. The stakes are incredibly high. You have to get that Clam to open up!

Listen to me, my dear, well-meaning Crowbars. If you push too hard, three things will happen. And they're all bad.

The First Bad Thing

First, you've hit his control alarm; and true to his nature, he closes up tighter. You actually make it more difficult for him to respond. He will instinctively shut down. If he knows you really, really want closeness, he'll stiffen up all the more. He sees it as a contest, a power struggle, in which he feels he has something to lose. And he intends to win in this struggle.

Ladies, think about it. How many times have you gone to the man with a very important request—for example, to discuss an issue vital to you, or to ask for his input on something about which you feel deeply— only to be turned down cold? Maybe you were crying. Maybe you were literally shaking with rage. Maybe your voice was raised. With a man, the sad truth is that the more you want something, the less chance you'll get it. Crazy, isn't it? And unfair to you.

If you don't give up but continue to try to get what you want, he will continue to deny you. But if you *do* give up, if you throw away your crowbar, if you accept that it's not going to happen, something amazing happens. What happens? Released from his control mode, his need to protect himself, the man will often come back to you and give you what you want!

The Second Bad Thing

The second bad thing that happens when you push too hard is that your intensity becomes the issue rather than what you are asking for, which is the main thing to you. You are asking for closeness. That's a perfectly reasonable and important request. But if you ask him with too much intensity, your desire for closeness is completely lost in the interaction. Believe me, closeness is the last thing on the man's mind as the crowbar bangs against his clamshell. He feels he is under siege! "Mayday! Mayday! This lady is trying to kill me! Or worse, she's trying to control me." He's not even aware of why you're so intense, just that you are intense.

As you pepper him with questions or urge him to talk to you, he is thinking a number of unflattering thoughts: "I gotta get out of here." "How can I get this screaming meemie off me?" "Wow! She is way too angry." "What a nag!" "She's out of control." "How dare she use that tone with me!" He won't express these thoughts to you, but he's thinking them.

I know what men think inside because—besides being a man—when working with them in marriage therapy sessions, I can get men to tell me what they are thinking.

How do I get them to do this? Often, I'll allow the woman to do her usual Crowbar routine. Then, after a few minutes, I'll ask the man what's going on in his head.

The woman is usually shocked to hear the defensive internal dialogue going on in her husband's mind. She doesn't realize how intense the man perceives her to be, and how massively turned off he instantly becomes.

The Third Bad Thing

Third, ladies, when you press too hard, you suffer damage personally. You become increasingly more resentful, depressed, and hurt. Your self-esteem and confidence drain away. Because you want closeness so badly with your man, it's easy to make it the focus of your life. While understandable, this is a big mistake.

I've talked to many women who have been broken by constantly throwing themselves against the Clam. They have made their number one goal getting the man to open up. It is often their only goal in life. Their frustration, disappointment, bitterness, and stress level are all through the roof. The result can be a variety of debilitating psychological and physical problems.

Part of my job as a psychologist is to convince these Crowbars that there is more to life than their single-minded pursuit of opening a Clam. I tell them they are creating a "triple whammy." First, their intense approach is doomed to fail. Second, if this is their number one goal in life, then they will experience failure, because they will never reach it. Third, they will suffer the same psychological and physical problems as battle-weary veterans of a losing war.

Ladies, please believe me when I tell you that any direct approach with a Clam will never work. Unless you enjoy being a martyr and wasting your life, drop your crowbar, and back away . . . slowly.

Control will always be inside a Clam—always. You can't get rid of it. It is a God-given trait in most men and all Clams. You can't make him open up. He has to *decide* to open up.

Pull Back from the Man

You are too close to the man, conversationally speaking. It is time to create some space. How do you feel when someone gets too physically close to you in a conversation? The close talker is invading your personal space, and you are uncomfortable!

You can feel her breath and know exactly what she had for lunch. When this happens, you back away to a comfortable distance, don't you?

The same thing happens when you get too emotionally close in a conversation with your man. You are invading the man's personal airspace, swinging your crowbar, so he naturally moves away from you emotionally.

You need to be the one to move. You don't pull back too far. You don't ignore him. You don't go quiet and say nothing. You move away just enough to give you both some room to maneuver.

If in Doubt, Ask

To create the right amount of space in your conversations and stay out of Crowbar mode, I want you to do two things. First, sit down with your man in a private place. Ask him to describe what you do and say when you're being a Crowbar.

Get from him a list of your specific Crowbar behaviors that cause him to stay shut: tone of voice and volume, body language, level of intensity, number and type of questions you ask . . . Building this detailed profile will help you avoid being a Crowbar.

Second, at least once in every conversation, ask him if you are exhibiting any Crowbar actions. Ask, "Am I being a Crowbar?" or "Do you feel pressured by me to open up and talk?"

If he says yes—and he will often say yes early on in this process of change—ask him what you are doing to be a Crowbar. Getting this information will enable you to stop the Crowbar behaviors and restart the conversation.

Not pressuring him to open up is an essential, foundational communication skill every Crowbar has to master.

In the next chapter, I'll cover an essential communication skill every Clam has to master.

ASK YOURSELVES THESE QUESTIONS

1. Crowbar (whether you are a man or a woman), are you willing to accept half the blame for the lack of conversational intimacy in your relationship?

2. Crowbar, at what point in a conversation do you begin escalating and getting too intense? What triggers you to wield your crowbar? What happens when you beat on the Clam and try to open him up?

3. Clam, when she is peppering you with questions and trying to pry you open, tell her what you are thinking. When she is doing this, what do you say and do?

4. Wife, can you relate to the Third Bad Thing that happens when you press him too hard, i.e., it causes personal damage to *you*?

5. Madam Crowbar, what will be the hardest thing about backing away and not using your crowbar in conversation?

CHAPTER 5

MEN,
YOU GOTTA LISTEN!

HERE'S A DIALOGUE I'VE HAD WITH hundreds and hundreds of men in my therapy office:

> **Man:** Doc, my wife talks a lot. The number of words just overwhelms me.

> **Me:** I know.

> **Man:** She jumps from topic to topic, and it's hard to keep up.

> **Me:** I know.

> **Man:** She gets very emotional and intense, and I don't know how to handle that.

> **Me:** I know.

Man: She picks the worst times to talk to me: when I'm watching a ball game on TV, right when I get home from work, at bedtime when I'm falling asleep, during sex . . .

Me: I know.

Man: I try to listen but usually get distracted and frustrated.

Me: I know.

Man: She says I don't listen to her. She says I'm not interested in her. She gets angry and hurt, and then I have to hear about that.

Me: I know.

Man: What's the deal? What am I supposed to do about this?

Me: The deal is: She's right. You're not listening to her. Not in an effective, loving way. But I can teach you how to listen in the right way.

Just as women (Crowbars) need to take responsibility for their part in the communication breakdown, men (Clams) need to assume their responsibility. A big part of male responsibility is their inability to *listen* effectively.

Men Are Lousy Listeners

By nature, by upbringing, and by cultural education, most men become lousy listeners. At least when it comes to listening to their women. Men can listen very successfully at work, with other men, to sports on television, to news, to YouTube videos on home improvement projects . . .

But when their girlfriends, fiancées, or wives speak, it's a different story. Suddenly, they can't listen. The most important person in the world to him is talking, and yet the man is unable to focus and understand what she's saying. It's as if she's speaking a foreign language to him. In a way, she is.

Listening to Your Woman Is Tough

Men, I know how difficult it is to listen to your woman. I've been married to Sandy for more than thirty years, and I have three (yes, three) *daughters*. They all like to talk. A lot.

As the girls grew up, I can honestly say there was never a moment of silence in our home during the day. If they weren't sleeping, they were talking.

Your woman uses many words, doesn't she? She tells stories with incredible detail, going from topic to topic; and she often gets emotional. I know it's very challenging to stay focused and be able to concentrate on what she is saying.

The bad news is, if you don't listen well, she will feel rejected. She will not feel loved by you. She won't be happy. And you know that if she isn't happy, you ain't gonna be happy either.

The good news is, you can learn how to listen to her in a way that will make her feel loved, understood by you, and close to you. I'm going to teach you how.

Here are my seven steps to effective, keep-your-woman-happy listening.

Step One: No Distractions

Believe me, it will take all your powers of concentration to listen to your woman. She can do two or more things at a time. You can't.

You can't allow any distractions. None. No television. No radio. No smartphone. No electronic device of any kind. No kids. No pets. No music. No squeaky chairs. No reading materials. No other activities.

Just you and her in a private, quiet place. (More on this in the next chapter.)

Step Two: Maintain Eye Contact and Attentive Body Language

Women are really into eye contact. Your woman expects and needs you to look into her beautiful eyes when she is talking. For her, eye contact is a part of connecting. Also, don't fold your arms across your chest or turn away from her in the slightest way. Always face her in an open, relaxed manner.

Step Three: Reflect Content and Emotion

Do not—I repeat—do not listen to her in silence. You could actually be understanding everything she says, but it won't make any difference if you stare, saying nothing. She'll think you're not listening and she'll follow this chain reaction: She'll talk more and repeat herself, she'll get frustrated, she'll get angry, and she'll feel hurt. All bad, obviously.

She needs to know you are listening, and she needs ongoing, periodic responses to what she is saying. When you reflect, that is, "cast back" to her what she is saying, you get both of these jobs done.

As she talks, you feed back to her some of her key words and phrases that will communicate understanding of what she is saying (content) and what she is feeling about what she is saying (emotions). You don't repeat everything she says; just say back enough to let her know you "get" what she's saying and feeling. Here are a few examples.

- "Waiting an hour at the doctor's office? I don't blame you for being mad."

- "Your friend Mary insulted you? I know that hurt you."

- "No raise again? Incredibly frustrating and discouraging."

If you are not accurate in reflecting back her thoughts and feelings, she will correct you. That's fine. Let her do it. In addition to building understanding, reflection is a great way for you to maintain your focus in the conversation.

Step Four: Ask Questions

Good listeners ask questions. And your woman loves questions. She's always asking questions, isn't she? When you're talking to her, it's the Spanish Inquisition! So return the favor when she's talking.

- "How do you feel about that?"
- "What do you think your friend will do now?"
- "What type of dog was it?"
- "Who else was at the meeting?"
- "What did you have for lunch?"

Questions show that you're interested and trying to get a full picture of the experience she's talking about.

Step Five: React Emotionally

Okay, this will be the hardest one to do. As a Clam, you are not known for your emotional reactions. You almost always have a logical reaction to what she is saying. But what your woman needs is your *emotional* reaction to what she is saying.

So keep your logical reactions to yourself, and try to feel a piece of what she is feeling. Reflecting her emotion—saying back to her what she is saying she is feeling—is good, but *feeling* some of it is better. Try hard to walk in her shoes, and imagine how you would feel if you experienced what she has experienced.

This is called *mirroring* her emotion. If she's angry, you're angry. If she's sad and hurt, you're sad and hurt. If she's happy and excited, so are you. You will never feel 100 percent of her emotion, but you can get to 10 or 20 percent.

Another avenue here is feeling your own emotional reaction to what she is saying. That's okay too, and she will appreciate your response. For example, she may be sad in telling you about a family member who rejected her. You can reflect her sadness but also share that you are angry at the family member for treating her badly.

Step Six: Allow Yourself to Be Called Out

Despite your best efforts, there will be times when you do not listen well. Or, for whatever reason, *your woman thinks you are not listening well*. Give her blanket permission—in every conversation—to inform you when she senses you are not listening.

Believe her when she calls you out. Don't get defensive. Don't try to convince her that you were listening intently. Accept her opinion and say, "I'm sorry. What was I doing that made you think I wasn't listening?" She'll tell you, and you can prove you were listening despite your signals to the contrary. Or if you truly weren't listening, admit that and apologize, then ask her to say it again.

Step Seven: Ask Her if She Thinks You're Listening

As you begin this process of learning, ask her this question at least once in every significant conversation: "Do you think I'm listening well?" This shows her that you are making a real effort. She will like that.

If she says yes, that's great, and you just move ahead in the conversation. If she says no, ask her what you were doing to convey the impression that you were not listening. Accept what she says, apologize, and make the corrections. If you were really listening, your behavior still made her think you weren't. So you will work to eliminate those non-listening triggers.

I also recommend that you sit down in a private place and ask your woman to describe your behaviors that make her feel you are not listening. Get from her a list of specific behaviors, then work hard to correct them.

The Benefits of Listening

Mr. Clam, when you listen well and comprehend what your woman is saying, here are some of the benefits:

- She feels you are interested in her and in her life.

- She feels loved.

- She talks less.

- She feels closer to you (and vice versa).

- You get drawn into the conversation.

- You get prepared to give a personal response to what she is saying.

These foundational skills, the Crowbar backing off and the Clam listening, will make a huge difference in your conversations.

Next, you need a place to *practice* these skills. I call this place a Couple Talk Time.

ASK YOURSELVES THESE QUESTIONS

1. Husband (or whoever is the Clam), are you willing to admit you are not a good listener when your partner is talking?

2. Ask your spouse how she rates you as a listener.

3. What makes listening to her difficult for you?

4. Which of my seven steps for effective listening will be the hardest for you to implement? Why?

5. Are you willing to let her call you out on poor listening during a conversation without objections or defensiveness? Are you willing to ask her, at least once in a conversation, if she thinks you are listening well?

CHAPTER 6

MAKE TIME TO TALK

HERE'S A DIALOGUE I HAD WITH a couple in my office. It's a dialogue I've had with many, many couples over the years of my practice:

Wife: We are pulling further apart. We're not close. We don't have much emotional intimacy. Can you help us?

Me: Let me ask you a question. How much time do you spend each week talking, in a private place in your home, just the two of you, with no distractions?

Husband: Does it count as a conversation if one of the kids is in the room?

Me: No.

Wife: Does it count if the television is on?

Me: No.

Husband: Does it count if one or both of us are on the phone?

Me: No.

Wife: Does it count if we text each other during the day?

Me: No. It has to be together, in person, in the same room in your home.

Husband: [After a brief discussion with his wife] Well, I guess it would be about ten minutes total. Maybe.

Me: Ten minutes isn't nearly enough time. Ten minutes is why you are pulling further apart. It's why you're not close. It's why you have little, if any, emotional intimacy.

Want Some Quality Time, Baby?
For a man (a Clam), here is what quality time with his woman looks like:

- watching a TV show together
- him watching TV or playing a video game or watching a video on his smartphone with his woman in the same room
- him watching TV or playing a video game or watching a video on his smartphone with his woman in the next room
- him watching TV or playing a video game or watching a video on his smartphone with his woman somewhere in the house
- watching a movie in a theater together

- riding in the car together in complete silence

- riding in the car together with the car radio on

- sleeping in the same bed all night

- sleeping in separate bedrooms all night

He is absolutely dead serious about these experiences being quality time. Just having you with him—or in the same vicinity—makes him feel content and peaceful. He actually feels close to you. All is right in his world.

The real beauty of this point of view is that no conversation is needed. In fact, he believes conversation will disturb his wonderful feeling of contentment. Conversation is hard work, and he just wants to be in your company.

If only his woman felt the same way, his life would be heaven on earth. Unfortunately, she doesn't. For a woman (a Crowbar), here is what quality time with her man looks like:

"It's just the two of us, in a private and quiet place, talking. And not just talking. Talking on a deeper level. Sharing our personal thoughts and feelings about a variety of topics. Opening up and revealing who we really are inside."

(Drum roll, please.) Whose definition of quality time together is the best one? I don't think my answer will shock anyone. I'm going to go with the woman on this one.

I know what you Clams are saying: "Oh, no! This is what she wants? I'm not good at this kind of deep, intimate conversation. Isn't there something else I can do to give her quality time? How about if I paint the house and she watches?"

The bad news is, your Crowbar *needs* deeper conversation to feel close to you and to feel loved by you. The good news is, I can help you learn—both of you—how to develop deeper conversations.

Both of You Need Emotional Intimacy

The man and the woman have the same need for emotional intimacy. The woman is just much more aware of her need. A good man who loves his wife will do the work necessary to meet her need in this area. He'll start the process with the mind-set *I'm doing this for her.*

Along the way, as he and his woman connect in conversation, he'll realize that *his* need for emotional intimacy is being met. It will dawn on him what he's been missing.

What Is a Great Marriage?

A great marriage is not paying bills and saving enough money for retirement. A great marriage is not raising healthy, successful kids. A great marriage is not taking care of the chores. *At its heart, a great marriage is a series of great conversations.*

Four Thirty-Minute Couple Talk Times

There are seven days in a week. Sit down together each weekend and schedule—placing the times on the calendar and in your phones— a thirty-minute Couple Talk Time on four of the days of the week. The man should be the partner who schedules these meetings and, when it's time for a meeting, invites the woman to join him for the thirty minutes. The Bible is clear that the husband is the leader in the relationship (see Ephesians 5:22-24), so it's his job to schedule and invite.

Have these meetings in a private, quiet place in your home. If you're not married, you can meet in one of your homes. It will be just the two of you, with no distractions. Get your small kids in their bedrooms. If you have teenagers, they will already be in their bedrooms because they hate you.

No pets. No TV, smartphones, or any other electronic devices in the room with you. After the first few Couple Talk Times you'll feel more comfortable with this process, but at first the Clam might be afraid the Crowbar will hold him captive forever, given the chance. Trust me, that won't happen, but if Mr. Clam feels safer setting a timer, go ahead and set the kitchen timer for thirty minutes before you begin.

Use a warm, fuzzy, comfortable place where you can relax and not be bothered by anyone or anything. The one hard-and-fast rule about these conversations is: Keep them positive and pleasant. Allow no conflicts in these Couple Talk Times.

Why Do You Need Couple Talk Times?

It is in these four Couple Talk Times that you will connect on a deep, emotional level. This kind of deep connection cannot happen at any other time during the week. You know why. Life is a blur of intense activity: your jobs, your kids, your chores, your family and friends, your bills, your church . . .

Outside of these Couple Talk Times, your conversational interactions—in person, on the phone, via text or e-mail—are superficial. Emotional intimacy *can begin* with one of these superficial dialogues, *but you will get deeper only in a Talk Time.*

Real intimacy requires privacy and dedicated time. Real intimacy is intentional. To achieve real intimacy, your actions must be calculated, planned, premeditated.

Most couples, several years into their marriages, begin to consciously avoid each other. Because they don't know how to get past the control/closeness roadblock, they begin living separate lives at home. It's easier and less painful to stop trying to connect in conversation.

Four thirty-minute Couple Talk Times will ensure that you stop avoiding each other and will provide the opportunity to genuinely begin the process of building great conversations.

Plus, the Clam can deal with a thirty-minute conversational period. He cannot handle a long, seemingly never-ending monologue from his woman. Without these Couple Talk Times, the Crowbar stores up a ton of material. When she gets her chance, she will unload all of it on the man.

She'll talk for more than thirty minutes, and he will get drowned in her avalanche of words. He'll zone out, show his impatience, or leave the situation.

Do these Couple Talk Times as early in the evening as possible. The later you put it off, the more likely something will come up, and you won't have this special time. Also, you won't be as fresh as you can be.

After a Couple Talk Time, you can do anything you want—even separately—for the rest of the evening. It makes no difference, because you have already had your emotional connection.

Excuses, Excuses, Excuses

Over the thirty years of my career as a psychologist, I've heard many excuses from couples for why they can't set aside thirty minutes four times a week. Here are the top eight excuses I've heard, along with my responses:

Excuse One: I want our emotional intimacy to be spontaneous, not planned.

David Clarke: Really? Dream on. If you have even one child, you can kiss spontaneity good-bye. Even without kids, deep conversations don't happen spontaneously. Couples who try to be spontaneous rarely, if ever, have deeper talks.

Excuse Two: I think we can do these four talks without scheduling them. They'll just happen naturally.

David Clarke: What will happen naturally is you won't do any talks at all. That's what has been happening. Isn't that right? If you don't schedule Talk Times, you won't do them.

Excuse Three: We talk enough during the week.

David Clarke: You're talking, but your communication is all superficial. That's not surprising or unusual, as you are working, running a household, attending to your children—there are so many parts to your lives. If you want more depth, you need the Talk Times.

Excuse Four: We're just too busy to do these Talk Times.

David Clarke: Baloney. We always make time for the activities that are important to us. I've never met a person who wanted to stay alive who didn't make time for such things as chemotherapy sessions, kidney dialysis, or insulin injections. If you don't make time to talk, your relationship will die.

Excuse Five: After work, running the kids around, supervising homework, chores, and doing dinner and cleanup, we're too tired to talk.

David Clarke: Poor babies. How old are you? Ninety? Get the kids to bed on time, and put off chores until later or move some to the next day when you do not have a Talk Time scheduled. The Talk Times will revitalize you both and pump new energy into your relationship.

Excuse Six: Why do we have to have four Talk Times in a week? Why not one or two?

David Clarke: Because intimacy is progressive. Each Talk Time builds on the previous one. By the fourth Talk Time, you will get to a deeper level.

Excuse Seven: The thought of sitting down for thirty minutes and talking to my spouse freaks me out. It'll be awkward.

David Clarke: Yes, it will be awkward and uncomfortable at first. You are out of practice. But it won't take long to get the hang of it and enjoy it. Trust me on this.

Excuse Eight: We'll just sit there staring at each other. What are we going to talk about?

David Clarke: Don't worry. I'll teach you exactly what you're going to talk about and how to talk about it.

Next, I'm going to show you what to do in these four Couple Talk Times.

ASK YOURSELVES THESE QUESTIONS

1. Which of you agrees with the Clam's definition of "quality time"? If you're the Clam, are you willing to consider and accept the Crowbar's definition of quality time?

2. In your typical week, how often do you communicate, how do you communicate (in person, text, phone, e-mail), and how deep is the conversation?

3. Which of my eight excuses will you tend to use to avoid these Couple Talk Times?

4. What do you think has the best chance of stopping you from scheduling and doing the Talk Times?

5. Are you both willing to commit, right now, to doing the four Couple Talk Times each week?

CHAPTER 7

TO KILL A PATTERN, INTERRUPT IT

I HAVE AN ANNOYING HABIT. Actually, I have more than one, but space doesn't permit me to describe all of them. This habit is one I've had for years, and it is so ingrained I don't even know when I'm doing it. Unfortunately, it drives my dear wife crazy. Right up the wall.

I hum and sing, over and over and over, the last song I hear. I may have heard it on the radio or the television. Of course, I never know the whole song. That's the really annoying part. I hum a few bars and sing the five or six words I remember . . . over and over.

It could be a country music song—I like country music. It could be a Christian song—at least that would make me seem more spiritual. It could be a song I hate, like "(I Can't Get No) Satisfaction" by the Rolling Stones.

I hum and sing my tiny remembered fragment until I hear another song, and then I start over with that one.

My twenty-two-year-old son, William, was visiting from college, and he was humming and singing—over and over—part of a song. I thought it was hilarious! Sandy failed to see the humor. She gave me a mean look and said, "Look what you've done."

I could have replied, "At least he isn't a drug dealer or a serial killer!" I didn't bother, since I was in enough trouble.

Sandy's Campaign for Sanity

Sandy began an anti-humming campaign. She made it clear that either I stop the habit or she'd have to kill me. I thought she was joking, but the look on her face made me wonder.

Since there are no rehab programs for annoying hummers (and believe me, Sandy tried to find one), we tackled the problem ourselves. First, I made the decision to stop humming. However, just knowing I was annoying her and deciding to stop weren't enough incentives to break the habit.

The humming continued. So the second idea was for me to catch myself humming and stop. Great idea in theory, except for one small problem: I didn't even know I was doing it. How can you catch yourself humming when you don't know you're humming?

One final idea has been the solution. Sandy verbally points out my humming to me. Sometimes she's even nice about it. When she interrupts me, I realize what I'm doing and can stop. I still hum, but not nearly as much.

Our marriage is saved, and my life is spared.

Embrace the Control-Closeness Problem

As you sit together in your Couple Talk Times, working to build emotional intimacy, expect there to be a tug-of-war between the Clam, who wants control, and the Crowbar, who craves closeness and intimacy. I call this the control-closeness problem. Believe that it will happen. Accept that there is zero chance it won't happen.

Embrace the control-closeness problem and the truth that it will happen over and over again. It is deeply entrenched in your conversational pattern and will occur until the two of you—working together—kill it. You kill it by following these steps:

- Admit you're doing it.

- Take a break.

- When both of you are ready, sit down again to talk.

- Build a conversation the right way.

Here's how to intentionally murder your control-closeness enemy.

Verbal Interruption

To battle the control-closeness problem, the technique of verbal interruption is the first idea I suggest. It won't be enough on its own, but it's a key part of the solution. Both partners agree to verbally bring up the control-closeness problem when it occurs in conversation. In other words, you catch yourselves in the act!

A very effective way to break an entrenched pattern is to point it out when it is happening—or as soon as possible. Ideally, you both agree this pattern is hurting your relationship, and you team up against it. This way you bring the automatic—the unconscious—behavior into the open. As long as this pattern stays hidden, you're dead. It retains its harmful influence. It will always win, and you will always lose.

If you don't speak up and point out the control-closeness problem when it appears, you are doomed to play out the same old Clam-Crowbar scenario.

What's Happening in Your Partner?

Because you can seldom catch yourself doing something habitual, especially when you are throwing a roadblock in your conversations (like humming, for example), I want each of you to point out this control-closeness problem when you see it happening in your partner. While most often we are unaware of when we are doing this, almost always we can see it in our partner.

Catching your partner erecting a conversational roadblock will work, as long as you are very careful in your approach. Tread softly, and be gentle. No sarcasm, critical tones, or arrogant attitudes are allowed. Unless you want to make a bad situation far worse, you work toward "speaking the truth in love" as the apostle Paul teaches in Ephesians 4:15. Your attitude is not, "Gotcha! You're doing something wrong." Rather, your attitude is just the opposite: "Honey, you're doing something that isn't helping our conversation. Can we start over?"

Let me illustrate. When the woman sees the man start to clam up, she could say, "Bob, I feel as though you're going into control mode now. I want some closeness, and you're pulling away." This is better than saying, "I'm sick of you not talking. Talk to me! Talk to me now!"

It's a good idea to ask your man to give you a statement you can use when he's being a Clam. If it's his statement—the one he gave to you to use—chances are better he'll respond to it without being hostile and defensive. Agree on this statement before you are in a situation when you have to use it. Also, letting him tell you what statement to use allows him to remain in control. It is he who has decided how you will interrupt him. Remember: With a man, control is critical.

Here are some "stop the conversation" statements the man could ask his woman to use:

- "You're clamming up on me."

- "You're shutting down."

- "I can see you're in your Clam role now."

As for the man, when he sees the Crowbar in action and she's not catching herself, he needs to say something to stop her. Again, it's a good idea for the man to ask the woman for a statement he can use with her. Fair is fair. He could say something like:

- "You're pushing too hard for closeness."

- "You've got the crowbar out."

- "Your intensity is backing me off."

As you begin this verbal interruption procedure, it will be awkward and difficult. In fact, many times the control-closeness scenario will automatically run its course. It will happen so fast, it'll be over before you can interrupt it. One or both of you will recognize what happened afterward. That's all right. That's perfectly normal.

After a Conversation
When you realize that you fell into the control-closeness trap again, it's not too late to bring it up at that time. Better late than never. You can learn another lesson from an old control-closeness conversation, whether it happened twenty minutes ago or two hours ago.

Talk about what happened. "Honey, did you notice what we did this morning? It was the same old Clam-Crowbar thing that the brilliant Dr. Clarke describes in his book. Let's talk about it."

Then go back and briefly re-create the conversation. Examine how each of you responded to the other. If it was your partner who was acting the Clam or the Crowbar, say, "I should have used your statement and put us back on the right track." If you know you were acting the Clam or the Crowbar, say, "I fell into old patterns and didn't notice. Hearing my statement would have helped me stop." Admit the mistakes each of you made and apologize for them. Talk about how you could have communicated differently.

Finally—and this is important—try the same conversation again. See if you can do better. It's like getting back on a horse after you've fallen off. If you want to win this challenge, take a few minutes to think about what went wrong, and then jump back on the horse. This is how you bury the old, habitual, unhealthy pattern and build the new, healthy one. You learn nothing if you just attempt to move on and never revisit the old conversation.

So go back and discuss what you both did wrong. Start the conversation again, from the top, watching for the control-closeness routine. You need the practice. It will pay off. With enough repetition, you'll learn how to avoid the same old trouble; and you will actually complete a decent, meaningful conversation.

As you improve, you'll both get better at noticing what goes wrong. The time from the end of the conversation to when one of you realizes what happened that prevented you from getting to a good conversation will get shorter and shorter. Pretty soon, you'll be able to point out the problem during an actual conversation.

And don't get discouraged if you mess up in this learning process. Like all of us, you will never reach perfection in this life.

During a Conversation

It's easier to look back at an old conversation that didn't work than to handle the intensity of a current one. When you interrupt your partner in the middle of a conversation, it's more difficult to negotiate the process of examining mistakes and restart the conversation. However, if you both follow some basic guidelines, breaking into a conversation is a powerful way to improve communication.

First, just as when you're dealing with an old conversation, the partner who brings up the problem must be careful. Be gentle but firm. Use the corrective statement your partner has given you. Your goal is not to humiliate but to heal.

Second, the partner who is interrupted must show grace under fire. You need to believe that what your partner is telling you is the truth, that what you are doing is hurting him or her. When you are caught being a Clam or a Crowbar, be big enough to admit it. It's not pleasant to hear; in fact, it will make you mad. Choke back your defensive or offensive reply, swallow your pride, and agree with your partner. Unless you are married to a pathological liar or master manipulator, you *are* doing what your partner says you are doing. Don't fight about it: "You are being a Clam." "I am not." "Are too." "Am not." When you're called on your pattern, accept it with as much grace as you can muster: "Well, I don't like it, but if you say I'm acting like a Clam (or Crowbar), I guess I am."

Third, take a short break just after the problem is pointed out. Feelings are running high, especially in the partner who has been called on the conversational carpet. In the past, continuing without a break has only done harm and perpetuated the problem. Agree to take a five- to ten-minute break and then to come back and continue the conversation. Use the bathroom, get a drink, or go outside for some fresh air. This cooling-off period signals the *end* of the previous unhealthy conversation and the beginning of a new healthy, constructive conversation. The intensity level, especially in the partner who was interrupted, is lowered, and the two of you are prepared to start over.

The fourth and final step is starting the conversation again. Come back together after the break and talk about what just happened. You do this to kill the old pattern rather than feeding it and, more importantly, to reach a different level on which you can genuinely communicate.

For example, if she was taking the Crowbar approach, the woman could say, "I'm sorry for being a Crowbar. You're right. I was giving you the third degree. Honey, I just want to be close to you and know you and love you."

If the man hears this, it helps. It really does. Not only can he forgive her for doing the Crowbar thing, but he can understand *why* she was doing it. He doesn't have to feel threatened now, because she doesn't want control. *She just wants closeness.* The conversation begins again with a whole new frame: a man and woman trying to be close.

The man could say, "Sorry for clamming up. I felt pressured and, as usual, I shut down, closing you out. I do love you, but I find it hard to let you see what's inside. I don't really want to shut you out."

If the woman hears this, it helps. In fact, it goes a long way. He didn't clam up because he wanted to hurt or reject her, or because he doesn't love her. He clammed up because he felt pressured to reveal inner thoughts and feelings, and he has trouble sharing himself. The conversation begins again with the partners on a new, deeper level. Their new approach is to find a way for the man to share himself freely, without feeling forced to do it.

As you practice catching one another in the control-closeness mode, two very nice things will happen. First, you'll find that you follow this unhealthy pattern less often. Being aware of a problem and regularly interrupting its operation is effective prevention. Why get cancer and hope to recover, when you can prevent it in the first place?

Since we're not in heaven yet and nobody's perfect, you will continue to get caught in this control-closeness gridlock. But—and here's the other nice thing—with practice you will become skilled at handling it. When it happens, it won't stop you cold and ruin your day as it used to. You'll fix it and have a good chance to move on to that precious condition we all got married to experience: intimacy.

Where Do We Go from Here?

I know what you're thinking: "Okay, Dave, we will catch ourselves doing the control-closeness thing. We'll take a break. When we both say we're ready, we will come back together to talk about why our conversation got derailed. But then what? How do we talk in the right way?"

Starting with the next chapter, I'm going to teach you the

specifics of how to talk in the right way. How to create deep, intimate conversations.

Up to this point, I've told you what *not* to do. Now I'm going to tell you what *to* do.

ASK YOURSELVES THESE QUESTIONS

1. Of what annoying habit are you guilty?

2. Are you both willing to embrace the control-closeness problem and admit it is going to keep stopping your conversations?

3. Give your partner a brief statement to use when you're being a Clam or a Crowbar.

4. When your partner uses your approved conversational interrupter statement because he or she senses the control-closeness roadblock, how hard will it be for you to accept it with grace and patience?

5. Which of my steps will be the hardest for you to do?

    • Catching your partner doing the control-closeness thing?

    • Taking a break with no anger and not abandoning the conversation?

    • Coming back together and talking about what happened?

6. Why do you think this will be hard for you?

CHAPTER 8

WOMEN, USE ONE-WAY COMMUNICATION

You're sitting with your Clam in your Couple Talk Time place. You're ready to create some conversation. Not "shoot the breeze," not have meaningless chitchat. You've had enough of that in your relationship. You can do superficial, trivial chatter with anybody. You want deeper conversations with your man.

A Secret to Deeper Conversations

It took Sandy and me fifteen years to discover this secret. Once we found it and began using it, our conversations got consistently deeper and we got a lot closer. This secret is one-way communication. Here's my definition:

Sharing on a topic with your Clam in a brief, low-intensity way with no expectation of receiving an original response.

Let me break down this definition and explain its four elements.

Sharing on a Topic

In one-way communication, you are the one who starts the conversation. You are the one talking. Your Clam's job (as I taught in chapter 5) is to listen well.

I know I'm stating the obvious, but you—the Crowbar—will start many of your conversations with your Clam. This is perfectly normal and will be the case throughout your relationship.

You are more talkative, more expressive, usually more feeling, and have twenty or thirty topics running around in your head at any given time. Your Clam has exactly nothing in his head most of the time. I'm serious. There's nothing in there. At least, nothing that will lead to an intimate conversation.

So it's okay for you to start many of your conversations. What counts is *how* you talk to your Clam.

Brief

I know what you're thinking: *Brief? I don't do brief! I like to talk, and I have lots of words.* Long, detailed stories in a conversation don't work with most men. Never have, never will.

You can talk your head off with another woman, using all the details you want. She'll love it and respond with her own very large reservoir of words. Try this with your man, and he'll get overwhelmed, lost, and frustrated. And he'll shut down.

In one-way conversation, you talk in brief bursts about a topic. Two or three minutes, on a topic interesting to you, is a good rule of thumb. Give him the basic sketch, some details, and express your thoughts and emotions.

At the three-minute mark, you're done sharing on that particular topic. Stop talking and pause to see if he is going to give an original response and continue the conversation on that topic. By original response, I mean he shares what he thinks or feels about what you just said. Or he asks you questions about what you talked about. If he does not, wait a minute or two to see if he brings up his own topic. If that doesn't happen, move on to another topic (you have plenty of them) and talk about it for two or three minutes.

If your topic is more serious and meaningful to you, it's okay to talk about it for up to ten minutes. This gives you a chance to share more emotions and details. But if you go over ten minutes, your Clam won't be able to keep track of all the details. He'll lose concentration, get confused, and will not give a response.

With a more serious, intense topic, it's even harder for your Clam to listen and stay engaged with you. So don't go over the ten-minute mark. After ten minutes, follow the same procedure as with a two- to three-minute topic:

- Pause to see if he gives an original response.

- If he doesn't, wait to see if he brings up his own topic.

- If he doesn't bring up his own topic, move on and talk about another topic.

Low-Intensity Way

I've already discussed this in previous chapters, but I want to make sure you get it. It's that important.

When you're talking, you need to keep your emotions in check and your intensity as low as possible. I'm referring here to regular, we're-trying-to-build-a-deeper-connection conversation.

If you're angry or hurt because of something he's done or said, you can express your emotions fully and be as intense as you need to be. That's a totally different context. In no-conflict, day-to-day conversation, intensity shuts your man down.

So don't raise your voice. Don't use aggressive body language like waving your arms, leaning toward him and invading his personal space, or grabbing his arm.

Do not pepper him with multiple questions in an attempt to force a reaction to what you're saying. Asking him repeatedly what he thinks and feels will trigger his control mechanism, and he will clam up tight.

You may ask him one or two questions, at most, about each topic you are sharing with him. That's fair and reasonable. If he answers, great; it could actually result in your having a conversation on your hands. But if he does not answer your questions, drop it and move on to another topic.

You may be thinking, *How can I keep my emotions in check and my intensity low, when I get nothing back? I'm a woman! Emotional intensity is what I do!* I know, I know. I'm not suggesting that you become an emotional robot with an on/off button. Just work to keep your intensity lower than usual. As long as it's beneath your man's threshold, you're okay.

Ask your man to work with you as you talk. Admit to him that you know your intensity turns him off and that you are trying to approach him in a different way. Ask him to tell you if you're being too intense when you are talking to him. With practice, you'll learn just how intense you can be without shutting him down.

No Expectation of an Original Response

In your Couple Talk Times, your job is to share on a number of topics with zero expectation that he will respond with a verbal comment. If your expectations are at zero:

- You will automatically be less emotional and intense (which will help him listen and respond).

- You won't be upset when he does not respond (your getting upset shuts him down and is miserable for you).

- You give him the freedom and control to respond on his own terms (which is the only way he will respond anyway).

Embrace this mind-set in every private conversation with your Clam: *I'm going to throw out a variety of conversation topics. I'll ask him a question or two about each topic. He's not going to have an original response to most of these topics. He'll respond to some of my topics. It's up to him. It's his choice which topics he responds to.*

When I teach Crowbars this mind-set, almost universally they tell me, "But Dr. Clarke, if I don't expect a response, I won't get one!" I always reply the same way: "No, you're wrong. Trust me. *Not* expecting a response will get you more responses and more back and forth conversation."

Here is the crazy truth. If a Clam feels he has to respond, he won't. If a Clam feels he doesn't have to respond unless he chooses to, he will.

When your Clam's control mechanism isn't threatened because he knows he can choose which of your topics to respond to, he'll give more personal, original responses to what you're bringing up. He'll share what *he* thinks about what you're saying. He'll share what he feels about what you are saying. He'll share something from his life that connects with what you're saying.

Now you have a conversation that will go deeper!

Here's What I'm Talking About

In a Couple Talk Time, you throw out five topics on the conversation table. These topics are interesting to you, and you think any one of them could lead to a deeper, we'll-both-talk-about-it conversation. You don't know, and now—with my help—you don't care, to which of these five your man will respond and want to talk about further. You're leaving that up to him.

You talk about a funny phone conversation you had with a friend. He gives no response. You talk about a tense interaction you had with your boss. No response. You talk about your son's struggles with his math. No response.

He's listening and reflecting, but so far he's not giving an original, I-want-to-talk-more-about-this response. Undaunted, because your expectations are zero, you talk about your sister's poor relationship with her current boyfriend. He shows sympathy but does not want to go any deeper on that topic.

Finally, you bring up your daughter's fears about her upcoming dance recital. For whatever reason, he does choose to talk about this topic. It clicks with him, and he talks about a conversation he had recently with her about her dance recital fears. Then he talks about how he used to feel before his high school football and baseball games. This leads to both of you talking about your fathers and their high expectations for academics and sports and the pressure and fears this brought to you.

This is a deeper conversation! You arrived at this more intimate talk because you allowed him to respond to his topic of choice.

He may respond to the first topic you toss out. He may respond to the third topic. He may have no response to any of your topics, but later in the Couple Talk Time he will circle back to one of your topics and continue the conversation about it.

He may have no response to any of your topics in a Couple Talk Time. Zero. Nada. Zilch. Bupkis. But he may respond to one of the topics you talk about in your next Couple Talk Time. You never know what he will respond to.

And he thinks *you're* unpredictable! Well, you are. But so is he! You have no idea—and you will never have any idea—what topics will prompt a response.

Crowbars, you have to be very patient and create a no-expectation, low-intensity, conversational environment with your Clam. When you do this, your Clam will respond to a percentage of your topics, and real conversations will happen.

Crowbars, get ready to learn one more essential skill that will help your Clam open up and talk on a personal level.

ASK YOURSELVES THESE QUESTIONS

1. Crowbar, how hard will it be to be brief when you bring up your topics?

2. Ask your partner to tell you what you do that he interprets as your being too intense. Get specifics.

3. What will be hard about not expecting an original response?

4. Ask your Clam how important it is to him to be allowed to respond to the topics he chooses.

5. In your Couple Talk Times this week, practice tossing out a variety of topics for conversation and allowing the Clam to choose which one he prefers and to which he would want to respond.

CHAPTER 9

WOMEN, PRAISE AND PRAISE AND PRAISE HIM

I'M ABOUT TO MAKE AN ADMISSION that I could not have made the first fifteen years of my marriage to the Blonde. Oh, it was true, but I didn't have the guts to admit it—to myself, to Sandy, or to anyone else.

Are you ready? Here it is! *I desperately need frequent praise from Sandy.*

Receiving her praise is not icing on the cake; it *is the cake* for me. It is a requirement. When I use the word *need*, I mean need. Our marriage would continue without her frequent praise, but it would be only a shadow of what it could be. That's how vital her praise is to me and to us.

Frankly, I don't care about receiving praise from other people. Don't get me wrong. It's nice. It feels good. But it doesn't meet any deep needs. It doesn't change my life and what kind of husband I am.

Sandy's praise does.

The Impact of Sandy's Praise
Sandy's frequent praise (notice I keep using this word) makes me feel respected. It gives me energy and confidence. It boosts my self-esteem.

71

It provides me with big-time encouragement. It strengthens my love for her. It makes me feel closer to her.

Best of all—from Sandy's viewpoint—her frequent praise helps me open up to her in conversation. Why? Two reasons. One, when she praises my positive behaviors in our conversations, I strive to do more of these behaviors and to do them better.

Two, her compliments make me feel safe, secure, and completely confident in her love. Her praise motivates me to open my clamshell and let her in to hear what's going on in my mind and heart.

Why Men Need Praise from Their Women

Men need praise because we just like the attention, and we like the feeling of satisfaction we get for doing a good job. A pat on the back feels good. We like credit for doing things. That may be petty, but it's true. (It's a guy thing, okay?) We are externally motivated.

We also need praise because women are confusing to us and it's difficult to figure out what makes them happy. We need feedback in the form of words of approval for behavior that pleases.

If I do a job for Sandy and she says nothing about it, I have two reactions. I'm hurt and angry because I didn't get praised. I also think the job didn't mean much to her. If Sandy wants to keep me initiating and helping, she needs to praise me. It's still my responsibility to do these things for her, but praise makes it a lot easier.

Even the King Needed Praise!

Every man with whom I've ever had contact in my life, both personally and professionally, has had this same deep core need for his wife's praise. Her frequent praise.

Solomon, King of Israel, the most powerful and wealthy and wise monarch of his time, got tons of praise every day from all kinds of people. When you're the king, everybody tells you what you want to hear. This king of the greatest nation of the day needed the genuine praise of his woman.

Solomon needed the praise of the Shulammite woman, who most scholars believe was the bride in the Song of Solomon. And, boy, did he get it! There isn't one page of the Song of Solomon in which she doesn't lay a bunch of heartfelt compliments on Solomon. She praised him all the time!

What was the result of the Shulammite woman's praise? The same result a wife's praise produces in every husband: He felt secure, safe, confident, and closer to her, and he listened to her talk. And he opened up and expressed very personal information to her.

That's what I'm talking about!

Frequent praise is an essential part of my plan to open up your Clam. Your Clam still has to choose to talk, but when he's showered with praise, he's going to want to open up.

Praise Your Man in Every Area

I want you to praise your man—your Clam—in every area of his life and your relationship. Praise him for:

- working hard at his job

- successes at his job

- all spiritual behaviors: having a quiet time with God, attending church, going to a Bible study, attending a men's ministry event, praying with you, sharing his spiritual life with you . . .

- all the chores he does around the home

- all of his positive parenting actions: spending time with the kids, helping with their homework, driving them to school and to their activities, making the lunches, being involved in discipline, praying with them, leading family devotions . . .

- his physical attractiveness

- his positive character traits

- parts of his personality you appreciate

- any behavior you appreciate and want to encourage him to continue

Does this sound like overkill? It's not! It absolutely is not! Ladies, it's smart to develop the habit of praising your man when he does something—no matter how small—that you like.

You are teaching him how to love you and how to meet your needs. Don't assume he knows when you're pleased with something he says or does; tell him! Make him feel as though he did something good.

Praising him in all these areas will indirectly lead to improvement in his communication skills. Why? Because your praise gives him the confidence to work harder in the area of communication—an area he knows is a big weakness for him.

Praise Your Man for Any Movement in Communication

I also want you to praise him when he takes the smallest positive steps in the communication part of your marriage. Praise him when he:

- reads any part of this book on his own

- reads any part of this book with you

- answers an end-of-chapter question

- schedules a Couple Talk Time

- invites you to a Couple Talk Time

- listens well

- asks you if he's listening well

- asks you to call him on listening mistakes

- gives you an original response to one of your topics

- shares something personal from his life

What will your man do when you praise him for positive communication steps he takes? He'll continue these praised behaviors, seek to improve them, and do more of them. All to please you and to get more praise. That's what a man does when he is praised.

Next, let's look at one thing a man can do to make his woman happy and feel closer to him.

ASK YOURSELVES THESE QUESTIONS

1. Ask your man how you're doing in praising him.

2. Tell him why you don't praise him more.

3. Ask him how he feels when you don't praise him for something he does or says that is positive for you.

4. Ask him how he feels when you do praise him.

5. Ask him how, specifically, you can praise him. Ask him for which actions or words he especially wants your praise. Ask him what words and actions he wants *from you* when you praise him (e.g., "Thank you . . ." "You spoil me . . ." "That was thoughtful . . ."). A hug, a hand squeeze, a kiss, a pat . . .

CHAPTER 10

MEN, OPEN UP
YOUR CLAMS!

IF YOU LOVE YOUR WIFE (and I know you do because you are reading this book), you do difficult things for her. Things you really, really don't want to do. Things you would never do unless you were in a committed relationship with her.

For a personal example, because I love my Sandy and want to make her happy, I watch at least one Hallmark Channel movie each week with her. These Hallmark productions are the ultimate chick flicks. I'd rather take a beating than sit through one. But it makes the Blonde happy, so I man up and watch the sappiest, cheesiest love stories ever made.

Every Hallmark movie has the same plot. I'm not kidding. Here's the plot: To help her parents with their failing family business, a woman returns to the small town where she was raised. She plans to stay for only a short time because she has a big-city job and big-city fiancé.

Her fiancé is obviously a loser and not right for her, but, by golly, she's going to marry him. She meets a small-town man—often a guy she knew in high school—and they fall in love. This wonderful guy pitches in to help her save Mom and Pop's business.

Just when it looks as though she's ready to dump her big-city fiancé and choose the small-town man, a crisis occurs that ruins everything. Some ridiculous misunderstanding breaks up her and her small-town man. Or another favorite Hallmark crisis: She sees her small-town man embracing another woman. Of course, the other woman is his sister or his cousin or an old family friend. But our woman does not know that. All she has to do is ask him, but she's too proud to do that.

So what happens? The woman, brokenhearted, runs back to her big-city man. They marry and have a miserable life together. No. You know that doesn't happen. That would not be a Hallmark ending. She realizes that she can't marry her big-city man. She returns to the arms of her small-town man. He proposes, she accepts, and—guess what—everyone is Hallmark happy. Except me.

Two hours of my life gone. Two hours of intense pain. Many police departments are now using these Hallmark movies in their interrogations of hardened male criminals. Ten minutes into the movie, these thugs break and give up all their criminal secrets. Anything to make the police stop the movie.

Make Your Wife Very Happy

There's something I want you to do for your wife that is more difficult than watching a Hallmark movie with her. I know that's hard to believe. But this action is critically important to her and to your relationship.

When you pull this off on a consistent basis, you get four excellent results:

- Your wife is very happy.

- You are very happy, because she is very happy.

- The two of you are closer and more in love.

- She will feel loved and return that love.

What is this difficult thing I want you to do? *Start more conversations with your wife.*

Be a Conversation Starter

Don't panic. Your wife will start at least 75 percent of your conversations. She can't help it. Talking is what she does. When she starts a conversation, your job is to listen effectively and respond to those topics you find particularly interesting.

As I have covered in previous chapters, her talking and your listening and responding is a main avenue to deeper conversations. This will work.

But if she starts virtually all your conversations, that won't work. This gets old for her because she has to carry so many conversations. Eventually, it will wear her out. And it gets old for you because it's hard to listen and respond to all that talking. Eventually, you will wear out.

Plus, she wants and needs to know who you are inside. What you're thinking and feeling about the events, experiences, and persons in your life. What is inside is the real you, and she can't know the real you unless you start conversations with your original, personal material.

So I want—and your partner wants—you to start 25 percent of your conversations. This is another main avenue to deeper conversations.

Love Does the Difficult Things

God says love does the difficult things. Love is not required to do what is easy, what comes naturally. Love does what is hard and unnatural. Opening up and being vulnerable and sharing your personal stuff is certainly hard and unnatural.

God says it all through the apostle Paul in Ephesians 5:25: "Husbands, love your wives, as Christ loved the church and gave himself up for her." This is the highest possible standard of love.

Jesus Christ sacrificed everything, including His life, for us. He never gave up. He moved past every obstacle in His drive to love us. He is our example (see 1 Peter 2:21). We are to be just like Him as husbands. Are we up to it?

Starting Conversations Is Good for You, Too

Mr. Clam, talking to your woman cleans out your emotional system and reduces stress. When you flush out the day's troubles and hassles, it's like dropping a fifty-pound backpack. You'll be happier and healthier.

Regular personal expression with your woman will add years to your life. Do you know why men die, on average, eight years before their wives? Because they want to!

Okay, that's not true. Men *do* die at a younger age than women, and one major cause is that they hold things in. We stuff emotions and stress from fear, disappointment, failure, discouragement . . . and eventually die from the internal damage this lack of expression causes.

In addition to living longer, the real benefit of sharing personally is a deeper relationship with your wife. You will experience something most men never do: intimacy with a member of the opposite sex. You will create emotional intimacy, and that will flow naturally into physical intimacy.

How to Start Conversations

One highly effective tool for starting conversations is the *Pad*. Buy several writing pads, the small ones you can find in any drugstore. Keep a pad and a pen near you at all times. Keep a pad in your car, at work, and at home.

You can also use an electronic device: smartphone, iPhone, iPad, etc. Your phone is the best idea because it is with you all the time.

Your pad or phone is for jotting down events and feelings and situations that happen during your day. Right after something happens, record it if you think it might interest your woman.

It might be a strong emotion like anger, or frustration, or joy. It might be a stressful interaction with your incompetent supervisor at work. It might be a memory of something you and your wife did years ago. These experiences may seem trivial to you; they are not trivial to your wife!

At the end of any day, you will have a nice little list of things that happened to you. Talking about them opens a window into the real you, the inside you, the you your woman longs to get to know.

You need to write down these personal items as they occur. If you don't, you will forget them and have nothing to say that evening to your dear, long-suffering wife. She'll ask, "What happened today?" And like an idiot, you'll reply, "Nothing."

Unfortunately, you will be telling the truth. Most men simply cannot remember anything that happened thirty minutes ago. Their day is like a giant scroll rolling up after them, blotting out everything that takes place. Even if something dramatic happens, like his saving a child from a burning house, if it's not written down as I suggest, a man will not remember it.

Women don't need a pad. They remember everything, in minute detail, from their day. They can easily and quite automatically recall every single emotion and event that occurred from the moment they woke up.

When a man gets home from work, his day is over, and with it, all memory of what happened. He wants to relax and think about what he'll do that evening and the next day. The trouble is, most great conversations are built on what happened that day in the couple's lives. Guys: Use the pad or whatever electronic device you choose.

So here's how this works. It's a weekday evening. You have scheduled a Couple Talk Time for that day. You get home, kiss your wife's beautiful lips, and say, "I love you. What can I do for you tonight?" After doing your regular chores and the extra jobs you asked for, you invite her to sit down and talk with you.

You say, "Tonight, I'll start the conversation." When she faints from shock, use smelling salts to revive her. Then, referring to your pad (or phone or iPad), start sharing your original material. Tell her what happened to you today. You'll be in control, and she'll be happy, because you're sharing your life with her.

By the way, don't do what one man in a marriage seminar audience told me he wanted to do. He asked me, "Dr. Clarke, can't I just hand her my phone so she can read what I've jotted down?" I said, "No! Refer to your notes, but *talk* to her!" You can't help some people.

Ladies, Be Patient

Ladies, please be patient as the man learns. The first few times he uses the pad—maybe the first twenty-five or thirty times—his list won't be too impressive. The things he chooses to jot down won't be too deep or personal. "Went to the store and bought batteries." "Got a paper cut and thought to myself, *Wow! That's a bad paper cut!*" Give him time. He'll get better.

Praise him for his efforts. Give him only encouragement for the first month. Show you are pleased with what he tells you. Then gently—very gently—tell him the kinds of things you'd like him to jot down and tell you: emotions, information about people, job stress, his spiritual life, etc. Don't demand. Don't be critical. Don't bring this up during a conversation in which he's using his list. Wait a while, and then in a warm, loving moment, tell him what you'd like to hear. You might even write this in a note because that is not as threatening as in person.

You Clams are probably thinking, "Okay, Dave, I get that I need to start more conversations, and I see how recording personal things will help me do that. But what specifically do I record during my day?"

Even though your woman will let you know, over time, what she wants to hear, I'm going to give you a solid gold, can't-miss list of conversation starters in the next chapter.

ASK YOURSELVES THESE QUESTIONS

1. Men, what things do you find difficult to do for your wife? Have you ever watched a Hallmark movie with her?

2. Men, what percentage of conversations do you start with your woman? What makes it so hard to start a conversation?

3. Men, are you willing to start 25 percent of your couple conversations?

4. Women, tell him what it will mean to you when he starts more of your conversations.

5. Men, are you willing to use a pad or your phone to record personal items during the day?

CHAPTER 11

A CLAM'S TOP NINE
CONVERSATION STARTERS

I'M SITTING WITH A HUSBAND IN my therapy office. He's a genuinely good guy. He loves his wife, he works hard at his job, he's a good dad, he attends church, and he pays his taxes. Here's our dialogue.

Husband: Dave, my wife is a wonderful person. And I love her. But over the past few years, she has not been interested in making love. She loves me, but she doesn't want to make love with me. She avoids it. She says she's tired. She stalls and puts me off. And when she does agree, she goes through the motions. I know she doesn't want to be with me. When we're done, she jumps out of bed like it's on fire.

Me: Do you know something? You've just voiced the number one complaint of the husbands I see in therapy.

Husband: Really? Can you help me?

Me: Yes, I can. Give me an honest answer to this question: How often do you sit down with your wife and share personal things with her? Your feelings. Your thoughts. Your stresses and concerns. What's going on in your relationship with God. How you feel about your marriage.

Husband: Frankly, practically never. Once or twice a year? I'm a guy. I don't share personal things.

Me: That's why you're a guy whose wife isn't into sex. That's why she is closed to you physically. If you don't learn how to open up with her regularly, she cannot—literally cannot—open up to you in the physical area. I can help you learn how to open up with her.

Step to the Conversational Plate

Mr. Clam, you are ready to start more conversations with your woman. Twenty-five percent, to be exact. You can do this because—every day—you're going to use a pad or your phone to record personal information about your life.

In my therapy office, when I explain to a husband the need to record personal topics—experiences, reactions, feelings—I always get the same response: "Okay, Doc, I'll do it. But *what* do I record for her? What does my wife want to hear? What parts of my day will be of interest to her?"

For centuries, men have been asking a variation of this question, "What does my woman want to know about me?" The answer is: everything. "Everything" is obviously too general. You need specifics.

Over my thirty years as a practicing psychologist, I have developed a list of the nine areas of a man's life that hold genuine interest for his woman. I tried for a top ten, but I could come up with only nine.

Here are a Clam's top nine conversation starters with a detailed example for each.

Number One: Events

Bring up events that occur in your daily life. Your woman wants to know what you do during your day. When you get home in the evening, she asks you, "How was your day?" or "What happened today?" You usually respond with these lame, conversation-killing responses: "I don't know." "Nothing." "Not much."

Now, with your notes, you can describe what happened to you today. You wrote down what happened. Although you are trying to record events she may find interesting, go ahead and include mundane, trivial experiences. It's hard to predict what she'll find interesting.

Jot down notes about work meetings, errands you ran, traffic delays, and interactions with customers, clients, and business associates. Conversations with coworkers, friends, neighbors, and family will be particularly interesting to her.

EXAMPLE

"I went to the drugstore to get some toothpaste and had an interesting conversation with the lady at the checkout counter. She was upset because her teenage son had been in a car accident and his leg was broken. I mentioned how we can lean on God at very difficult times and that friends at church support us when life is hard."

This conversation could go somewhere. You've given your wife several avenues to pursue: car accidents family and friends have had, car accidents you and she have had, how you and she have relied on God when life has been painful, times she has invited others who are hurting to church . . .

Number Two: Current Stresses

I know you don't want to talk to your woman about your stress. Most men don't.

You prefer to handle it yourself. You don't want to upset her. You believe talking about it won't help.

Stuffing your stress and keeping it inside will harm you and deny your woman the opportunity to get to know you better. She wants to be on the same team and help you deal successfully with the stressful situation.

EXAMPLE

"My boss criticized me today in front of three coworkers. The worst part is, I did make a mistake that cost the company money. I felt guilty and embarrassed."

If you can get the above words out of your mouth, you are on your way to a deeper conversation with your woman. You can talk through exactly what happened, your reaction, the reaction of your coworkers, and what you can do about it. Your wife can support you, encourage you, and pray for you. Trust me, you'll feel better for getting it off your chest, and your wife will be thrilled that you confided in her.

Number Three: Strong Emotions

I'll bet your woman loves to ask you this question: "How do you feel about that?" You usually avoid answering or say, "I don't know." There's no way to build a decent conversation with these nonresponses.

Be proactive, and jot down the strong emotions you experience during the day—anger, frustration, joy, relief, fear, hurt, feelings of failure, disappointment, peace—and share them with her.

EXAMPLE

"I'm mad at my brother. Furious. He called today and said he would not contribute any money for the care our parents need. He told me we have more money, so we should take care of it. Talk about selfish!"

Talking about this honest expression of emotion could lead to a discussion of other times your brother was selfish, your conflictual relationship with him, and the family dynamics over the years. This is deep, personal stuff!

Number Four: Decisions

I spent years of our marriage thinking through decisions and figuring out what to do without ever talking to Sandy. I would inform her of my decisions. I hurt and insulted her by cutting her out of the process. And in doing so, I failed to have her wise input, which would have saved me from some dumb decisions.

For decisions big and small, tell her what you're thinking, and get her feedback every step of the way.

EXAMPLE

"Honey, I think we need to save more for our retirement and make some changes in our investment strategy. Let's spend a few weeks discussing and praying about this. I'll tell you what I think, and you tell me what you think."

These financial discussions, while not fun, will be important and bring you closer.

Number Five: Personal and Relationship Memories

As you go through your day, sometimes memories from your past surface: your childhood, family and friends, school, jobs, sports teams you played on, trips, joyful times, traumatic events, illnesses . . . Sometimes the memories will be from your relationship: when you met, your dating days, your honeymoon, vacations, funny events, children, moves, crises, or old friends with whom you used to be close.

EXAMPLE

"I was thinking of Bill and Patty today. Man, remember how close the four of us were? That one trip up the Columbia Gorge? Once we moved, we lost track of them."

This could be a fun walk down memory lane. You and your wife could share about the times you spent with Bill and Patty, what their friendship meant to you, and memories of other old friends from your past . . .

Number Six: Your Relationship with God

Your personal relationship with God, established when you trusted Jesus as your Savior, is the most important part of you. Telling her about it will let her see the real you. Don't keep your spiritual life a secret. Let her know about your quiet times and Bible reading, how you're applying the Bible to your life, spiritual victories and defeats, what you are praying for, your spiritual struggles and doubts . . .

EXAMPLE

"I have to be honest; the last few weeks I've been in a spiritual funk. I haven't had many quiet times, and when I pray, it doesn't feel like God is listening. I think I'm mad at God because He did not help me get that promotion at work that I was counting on. And He did not heal Bob, which really hurt."

This kind of sharing is very personal. Very vulnerable. It is a courageous step to be vulnerable. When you are open and honest like this, your wife will be able to support and encourage you. She may share times when she has struggled spiritually. There's no question this conversation will go deep. And she can help you work things out and get back on track with God.

By your sharing your innermost, most important thoughts and experiences, you will help her in her Christian walk. It will begin a lifelong spiritual bond between you. If you are not reading the Bible and praying together, talking about your relationship with the Lord could lead to regular devotions as a couple as well as individually.

Number Seven: What You Read and Watch

Everything you read (books, articles, online material, newspapers, blogs, magazines) and everything you watch (movies, television, online video clips) can lead to a terrific conversation with your woman.

EXAMPLE

"I watched part of a documentary on depression last night, and it hit me pretty hard. You've been telling me I'm depressed. Now I think you're right. I have a lot of the symptoms."

The documentary can be a catalyst for a series of deeper talks about your depression. About what may be causing it, how you feel, the impact it is having on your mate and your relationship, and what steps will get you out of depression. By allowing your woman into your private world and your concerns, you gain a powerful, caring, loving ally.

Number Eight: Evaluate Your Relationship

Your woman spends a lot of time thinking about your relationship. She'll love it when you talk about what you think about your relationship. This is one of her favorite topics. Share with her what you think are the strong areas, the weak areas, and what you believe you two can do to make the relationship keep getting better.

EXAMPLE

"Sweetheart, I don't think we do enough fun activities together. We used to Rollerblade and ride bikes, but it's been a while. Going out to eat or see a movie is good, but I want to do some fun, outside-the-box activities with you."

You both can talk about the fun things you did together in your dating and early marriage days, and how the kids and their needs caused you to drop these activities. You can brainstorm and come up with some shared activities and when you can do them.

Number Nine: Follow Up on Her Topics

Your woman will absolutely love it when you ask questions about specific topics she's interested in or that are important to her. This shows you care about her and her life. It will help you know her better too. And asking these questions will lead to deeper conversations.

EXAMPLE

So here's how you do it. A few days ago, she talked about her relationship with her mother. They had a difficult phone conversation that triggered a ton of painful memories and emotions. She spoke to you about her mom for ten minutes and went through a number of intense emotions: anger, hurt, frustration, confusion . . .

You know this topic is important to her, so you jot down a few follow-up questions about her and her mom. At your next Couple Talk Time, you begin with these questions.

"Honey, I've been thinking about you and your mom and the talk we had about her a few days ago. How do you feel about that phone conversation now? What else do you want to tell me about your mom and your relationship with her? What can I do to help you with your mom?"

This is conversational gold to your woman! Most men would avoid asking about an emotional, painful topic like this. But not you. You want to hear about it because it is important to her. Talking about it will make her feel better.

We've established a solid foundation for your conversational life together. But I'm going to take you even deeper. It's time to look at the incredible differences between your brains and how these differences block you in conversation.

ASK YOURSELVES THESE QUESTIONS

1. Which of these nine personal sharing categories will be easiest for you? Why?

2. Which of these nine categories will be the most difficult for you? Why?

3. Ask your woman what it will mean to her when you regularly start conversations.

4. Ask her which of these categories are most important to her.

5. Ask your woman if there are any other categories she'd like you to use in starting conversations.

PART THREE

We Need to Build Deeper Conversations Every Week!

CHAPTER 12

"WHAT'S THE MATTER WITH YOUR BRAIN?"

A MAN AND A WOMAN ARE in conversation. It's just the two of them. At first, everything's fine. There is eye contact and a comfortable feeling of closeness between them. Both are taking turns talking and listening.

What could go wrong? Well, since it's a Clam and a Crowbar talking, plenty.

Suddenly, it happens. The woman notices that the man is not listening. She sees all the telltale signs. His mouth is hanging open, and a small line of spittle is running down his chin. His eyes are glassy and staring off into the distance. His body is rigid. There is not even a twitch.

Is it a stroke? Some of kind of seizure? Have aliens invaded his body? No. It's what all women *hate*. It's what drives them crazy. It's *the Zone*.

The Male Zone

The "Zone" is a periodic mental blank spot that men move into without warning. During his time in the Zone, there appears to be very little—if any—brain activity. For a brief period, conscious thought ceases. The man is, for all intents and purposes, a vegetable.

The woman takes the Zone personally. She says, "You're not listening to me!" She is right. He's not listening to her. Now, the situation is bad enough at this point. The woman feels insulted and is angry because the man wasn't paying attention to her. But it gets worse.

The woman, being a woman, has to ask *this question*: "What were you thinking about just then?" The man, being a man, with all sincerity has to give *this answer*: "Nothing."

The woman can't believe it. "What do you mean, *nothing*?" She can't conceive of going blank and having nothing on her mind. It's never happened to her. She's convinced he's lying. He had to be thinking of something!

Men, in this situation, if we could just come up with something that we were thinking, it might help satisfy the woman. At the very least, it would be some damage control. Maybe:

"Funny you should ask. I was thinking of a cure for cancer."

"I was thinking of some way to achieve world peace, and I almost had it before you interrupted me."

"Honey, during that brief time when it looked as though I wasn't there, I was thinking how beautiful you are."

That last line would really work! Unfortunately, the man literally had *nothing* on his mind. Absolutely, completely, and—all kidding aside—nothing on his mind.

The Zone Is Normal, Though Annoying

Speaking on behalf of all men, ladies, let me assure you that the Zone is not an intentional attempt to drive you over the edge of sanity. It just seems that way. The Zone is a perfectly natural, normal part of being a man.

In fact, the Zone is a protective shutoff valve for a man's brain. When his brain is in danger of taking in too much information at one time—like when you're talking—it automatically shuts down. By doing so, his precious neural circuits are shielded from damage.

Ladies, do you believe that? Of course you don't. I thought it was worth a try. However, the Male Zone is an example of a very important truth. Men and women, Clams and Crowbars, think differently. Our brains are incredibly different, and so the way we think, the way we talk, and the way we process personal information are all different. And these differences block our communication. Over and over and over again.

Another Major Conversation-Killing Difference
In previous chapters, I've covered some big Clam-Crowbar differences that kill conversations. It's time to address another major conversation-killing difference. This one has to do with how men and women typically handle personal information about themselves—what they are inside.

Women are *external, relational processors*. Men are *internal, solitary processors*.

To develop deep, intimate conversations as a couple, you must understand this difference. Let me describe the three areas that make up these two diametrically opposed styles of processing.

Women Are in Touch, Men Are out of Touch
Most women are in constant touch with their personal, inside information: thoughts, feelings, reactions, pain, hopes, and dreams. Women know what's inside at all times. It's all just right there on the surface. When an event occurs, a woman reacts immediately, and she knows what the reaction is and why she reacted in the way she did.

Most men are not in touch with their personal, inside stuff. The good news is, men do react inside to events with thoughts, pain, and such emotions as pleasure, sadness, anger. The bad news is, they have no idea what their reactions are or why they come. Their personal responses are deep inside, and it takes time for men to locate them—and even more time to understand what they are and why they felt them.

Let's say a man and a woman have just seen a movie together and are walking out of the theater. It was a powerful, emotionally intense drama. A real tearjerker. The kind of movie women love and drag their men to see.

This woman's mind is filled with all kinds of thoughts, emotions, and reactions to the movie. The man's mind is a complete blank. For him, the movie is over, and he's thinking about what he'll order at the restaurant.

Women Share, Men Suppress

Women not only know what is inside them, but they naturally and spontaneously share it. It comes up and out. "I know what I'm thinking and feeling, and I'm going to tell you right now." They've been doing this all their lives.

Women can't stand to hold in what's inside. They have to get it out—and I mean all of it—as soon as possible. For women, an event really hasn't taken place until they've talked about it with someone else.

Men naturally and spontaneously suppress their personal information. It stays inside, where no one can see it. We don't show it to anyone. We've been taught to hold it in.

Most men have never seen another significant man in their lives ever share something personal. We learn as little boys that real men don't share personal things with anyone. The act of stuffing our feelings and reactions is an automatic reflex. Most of the time, we don't even realize we're doing it.

This stuffing way of life is great for war, business, and sports. But it's a disaster in a romantic relationship with a woman. A woman needs to hear what's going on inside this man she loves.

In our movie example, the woman—who is crying—starts sharing her reaction to the movie before she's even out of the theater aisle. She covers, in detail, what she liked about it, what she didn't like, her emotions, events in her life that the movie reminded her of, how the movie related to her relationship with her man . . .

She and her man are in the car halfway to the restaurant when she finishes. She asks the man a reasonable question: "What did you think of the movie?" You ladies know what's coming, don't you? The man replies, "I don't know."

The sad reality is, he is telling the truth. His reactions to the movie are buried deep in the vault and he can't—yet—identify them.

Women Wing It, Men Mull It Over

Women process as they talk. They make connections and figure out their reactions as they go. A woman has no idea where she'll end up when she starts talking, and she doesn't care.

"I'm just going to start talking, and let's see what happens. What am I going to say next? Even I don't know!"

She's asking her man to join her in her conversational adventure. She'll share a bunch of seemingly unrelated emotions and reactions and details about the movie. This is the shotgun approach to verbal expression, spraying out all the stuff that's in her head. And there's a lot of it.

Men do all their processing internally. It's a big secret. Before a man will share verbally what's inside, he'll go through a careful and private series of steps. First he has to find out what's in there. Then he'll chew on it. He'll mull it over. He'll think through it all twenty times. He'll organize it and collate it.

Finally, he has his response all figured out and put into concise and presentable form. Then he may—just may—decide to give it to his woman.

A man won't wing it in conversation. You'll never hear a man say, "Well, honey, I'm not sure what I'm feeling, but here goes." No way. He must go through his painstaking mental inventory every time.

He needs to. He's a man. He's a Clam. He won't blurt out something that might embarrass him. When he speaks, he knows what he's going to say. Very short on spontaneity and long on control.

Our movie woman verbally dumps a large amount of information and emotion about the movie. She spontaneously bebops around, tossing out all kinds of reactions. She verbally sorts out, over a fifteen- or twenty-minute time frame, what the movie means to her.

The man says very little, if anything, about the movie. Certainly nothing personal or specific. He doesn't know how he feels about the movie or what it means to him, his life, and his relationship with the woman. He has to take time to figure all this out.

Your Brains Are in the Way

Can you see how this difference in the way men and women process what they experience in their lives is killing your conversations? No matter what the topic is, the conversation can't get off the ground with these very different processes going on.

She knows her reaction to the topic. He has no idea what his reaction is. She expresses her reaction. He keeps his reaction inside. She processes out loud. If he processes at all, he does it internally.

Two very different brains operating on two very different tracks. If you're ever going to create deeper talks, you need to find a way to connect your brains.

I know the way to do that.

ASK YOURSELVES THESE QUESTIONS

1. How often does the "Zone" happen in your conversations? When it does happen, how do each of you deal with it?

2. Talk about the differences in how you process what you experience in your lives, and how these differences impact your conversations.

3. Take a recent conversation and discuss how your processing differences killed it.

4. Mrs. Crowbar, how hard is it to accept that your Clam's reactions to a conversational topic are buried deep inside him and not easily accessed?

CHAPTER 13

CONNECT YOUR BRAINS
WITH THE "TRAIN"

I LOVE TRAINS. Just ask the Blonde. Every time—and I'm not exaggerating—I see a train, I say to Sandy, "I love a train." Every time, she says the same thing back to me: "I know."

I love everything about a train. I love how a train looks. I love the seats. I love the sleeper compartments. I love the dining car. I love the motion as it sways from side to side. I love the way you can watch the countryside rolling by as the train hums down the tracks.

Just about every summer, Sandy and I go on vacation with our dear friends Bob and Pam Johns. And just about every summer, Bob finds a train for me. He locates trains in obscure little towns in Florida, Georgia, South Carolina, and North Carolina. Now that's a true friend!

What I love most about the train is the romance. When you board a train, you enter a sweet and powerful romantic world. As just one example, when we're on a train, Sandy can't keep her hands off me. Okay, that's not true.

She can't keep her hands off me, no matter what form of transportation we're using: car, bus, bicycle, golf cart, horse carriage . . . Okay, that's not true, either.

But what is true is that you and your spouse are going to love the train I'm about to describe to you. This communication technique I call the "train" has revitalized my marriage. How? By giving us consistently deep and intimate conversations.

The train will do the same thing for you two.

A Man Must Have His Train

Use your imagination and picture, in your mind's eye, a train station with a train stopped in front of it. You can see the station house, the wooden platform, and the long, dark line of cars. Smoke is billowing from the locomotive's engine. As the train prepares to leave, a man and woman are standing on the platform talking.

When the man feels the need to get some space and do some processing, he'll get on this imaginary train and go down the tracks some distance, alone. Notice, ladies, I said *alone*. You never get on the train with the man.

The trigger for the man boarding the train will be one of two things. One, *the woman asks him to share something personal.* Or two, on his own (miracles do sometimes happen), *he realizes the need to share personally.*

If he has to share something from inside himself, something below the superficial level of chitchat, he'll need to get on the train.

He'll use his time on the train to look inside and see what's there. He'll figure out his feelings and his personal reaction. He'll pull it all together into some kind of organized package he can understand. Then, when he's ready, he'll come back to the station, find the woman, and start sharing what he's found out.

"Are You Serious, Dr. Clarke?"

Now, I've presented an ideal picture. I can hear you ladies tell your stories:

"Really, Dr. Clarke? You cannot be serious!"

"I know all about the train. Tell me something I don't know."

"He's always getting on the train."

"He doesn't look inside when he's gone."

"He never comes back from his train trips."

"When he comes back, he doesn't share something personal."

"Who do think you're kidding, Dr. Clarke? Do you really expect us to buy this?"

Hang on, ladies. I'll address these concerns. They're all valid, I know. If you and your men each follow my train instructions, this new system of communication will work.

He Cannot Spontaneously Share What's Inside

What you need to understand now is that the man needs the train because he will not, he cannot, stand with the woman and process his inside stuff *on the spot*. This isn't a cop-out. He literally can't do it. God did not make him that way. And all his life his training has only solidified it.

Therefore, your typical man (Clam) has a delayed reaction to anything personal. He can talk spontaneously about sports, the weather, what power tools he'll use to fix the garage door, and what he wants for dinner. If the conversation gets any deeper, he's way out of his element and will clam up. If you try to force a reaction and get something deeper out of him, ladies, you know what will happen. He'll never—and I mean never—give you the personal stuff you really want. That's the way he saves face and maintains control.

Ladies, you can't expect your man to spontaneously share what's inside. You could get this from another woman, but you didn't marry a woman. A woman would have an immediate, personal response to anything you shared with her.

In fact, two women (Crowbars) can talk at the same time and

understand everything being said! Watching two women in a conversation is an amazing experience. They talk at the same time. They laugh at the same time. Both are sharing personal thoughts and emotions spontaneously, openly, and with complete freedom. Women have no need for a train.

There are no pauses. The air is filled with words—personal, deep, meaningful words. It doesn't even look like they're breathing!

Okay, that's how two women talk. It is a totally different story when a woman and a man talk. Ladies, you have a right to expect your man to share personally with you. Without mutual sharing, your relationship can't be deep and intimate.

What I'm saying is: You have to let him do his personal sharing his way. And his way is using the *train*.

To really connect on a significant level in conversation, both partners need to learn their individual roles in the train scenario. I have one set of guidelines for women and one for men.

Women and the Train

I know it's tough for you to understand the train. *You* don't need the train. You can talk at the drop of a hat. You're ready to process out loud all the time, and you usually do. Your problem is reducing the amount of verbal processing so you don't bury your man in an avalanche of words.

You say, "He just won't talk to me!" That's right, he won't. Not when you back him into a conversational corner. You've got to give him some space and time to process, to catch up with you in the personal information department. You've got to give him the right and freedom to use the train.

Let him do his processing in secret, inside. On his own. It's a covert operation. When he finds his personal reaction, he'll come back and share it with you.

Remember, he won't talk just because you want him to talk. He won't talk—not even a little bit—if he feels pressured by your impatient silence, body language, and questions. He'll talk when he's good and ready, when he's prepared. He'll talk to a woman who gives him space and time to process, who will patiently wait at the train station.

Men and the Train

Your job, Mr. Clam, is to learn to use the train in the right way. Get on the train, find out what's inside you, and come back and restart the conversation.

Don't board the train and never come back. I did this to Sandy a million times, and I know you've done it to your woman over and over. The train is not to be used to escape your woman. It is a God-given method for you to share personally with her.

It's time to stop the one-way train trips and start taking round-trips. I'm talking about a *loop train*—a train that forms one big circle around the city. No matter where you board the train, if you stay on long enough, it will come back to your starting point.

Come up with a phrase you can use to alert the woman that your train is leaving. "I'm getting on the train now." "Let me think about that." "I'm going to do some processing, and I'll get back to you."

Stating out loud that you're about to board the train puts your woman's mind at ease. She feels respected, knows you heard what she said, and can comfortably wait for your reply.

When you're ready to talk to her about what you've found inside, find her and continue the conversation. If it was a short train trip, it will be easy to find her. She'll be sitting in the car next to you, at your table in a restaurant, or beside you on the couch in your home.

If the train trip took longer, several hours or one day or more, you'll have to go out of your way to find her. However long your train trip and wherever she is when you're back, go to her and share what you've found.

For longer train trips, most often you will restart the conversation in your next Couple Talk Time (remember these Talk Times from chapter 6?).

The Pad idea I covered in chapter 10 will also serve you well in the train process. If your woman has talked about a subject important to her or interesting to you, use the pad or your electronic device.

In the presence of your woman, jot down the following: the subject, any questions she wants you to answer about the subject, and what she specifically wants you to comment on in your response.

Do you want real closeness with your woman? Do you want her to feel loved? Do you want real peace and companionship in the relationship? Do you want to avoid conflict with a disappointed or angry or resentful woman? Do you want the best sex you've ever had?

I know your answer to all these questions is yes (especially the last one). All of this can be yours if you use the train and in the right way.

Me, Sandy, and the Train

I love my wife, Sandy. I am a highly verbal, expressive man. I'm the last person to leave church, if that tells you anything about me. I am also a clinical psychologist, trained to help others identify and express their deepest feelings and secrets. In my therapy office and in my marriage seminars across the country, I teach couples how to communicate.

And guess what? I can't respond immediately in a personal way with Sandy in conversation. Ladies, if I can't do it, your man can't do it.

Once Sandy and I discovered the train idea, everything about our conversations changed. We could actually develop deeper, more intimate conversations. Through the years, the train has helped us become closer and more in love than ever.

I've introduced the train concept. Next, I'm going to show you exactly how it works in your conversational life.

ASK YOURSELVES THESE QUESTIONS

1. Ladies, can you accept that your man cannot spontaneously give personal reactions? Ask him if he needs the train.

2. Ladies, what will be hard about allowing him to use the train? Tell him this.

3. Men, how many times have you boarded the train and never come back? Why do you think you do that?

4. Men, try to explain to your wife how you do your internal processing.

5. Ladies, will you allow him to use the train?

6. Men, will you work hard to learn how to use the train?

CHAPTER 14

A GREAT TALK
TAKES A WEEK

You're thinking, *A WEEK? Are you serious?* Yes, I am. I want you to understand three truths about conversational intimacy.

You already know the first truth from the previous chapter on the "train": The man has a delayed reaction when it comes to personal sharing. So he needs time to process in order to get to a deeper level in a conversation.

The second truth is that the woman also needs time to process, so she can discover and express her deeper emotions and thoughts. Although she is much more aware of her personal information, it takes her a while to sort through it and find out what it means to her and her marriage.

The third truth reveals part of God's wisdom in creating marriage: The deepest and best kind of emotional intimacy happens when a man and woman react to each other in a conversation. It takes time to process our incredibly different reactions (about a week), but the result is worth it. The result is real closeness.

Intimacy Is Always Progressive

To achieve the conversational intimacy you want and need, you will need to have *a series of talks* on the same topic. No couple reaches deep, complete sharing on one topic in one sitting. It can't be done. It is not God's design.

Real intimacy is always progressive. It happens in stages. It cannot be deep sharing right away because the man needs time to process, the woman needs time to process, and the couple needs time to process together.

When you sit down together and talk about a subject the first time, that is a starter conversation. By its very nature, it is superficial. No depth. No real meaning.

In my plan (which I believe follows the teaching of the Bible), you two have to work together to get to a deeper level. And that happens over the course of about a week.

Let me show you how this progressive, over-the-course-of-a-week intimacy works. One caveat: I have the woman begin this first conversation. The man could start the conversation, but I go with the woman because women start 75 percent of opposite-sex conversations. And that's okay. It's just reality.

Your First Conversation

The first conversation could start anywhere. It could be in a scheduled Couple Talk Time. It could be in the car. It could be at a restaurant. Let's say this first conversation is in your first scheduled Couple Talk Time of the week.

The woman brings up a topic and talks about it. It's okay for her to share as completely as she wants to share. She shares what she thinks, what she feels, and her personal reactions to the topic. She shouldn't rattle on and on, because she might lose the man in her Niagara Falls of words. If she speaks for ten minutes or less, she's good.

What is the man doing as the woman talks about her topic? Staying silent? No. Trying to keep his eyes open? No. Interrupting her and bringing up something else? No. Zoning out? He'd better not.

As I covered in chapter 5, he is *listening*. He's not doing anything else but listening; he's got eye contact and good body language; he's reflecting her content and emotion; he's asking her questions about her topic; and he's trying to begin to react emotionally to what she is saying (he'll need the train to get a full emotional reaction).

As he listens well, some very good things happen: She feels loved because she has his attention; she can talk more freely and openly about her topic; she will be able to limit her number of words because she knows he's getting it; and he gets pulled into the conversation and gets warmed up and ready to ride the train.

During her ten minutes, it's also okay for the woman to ask the man questions about her topic and raise issues she wants him to comment on when he responds. She is careful to not pump him with a ton of questions, because that will overwhelm his listening apparatus.

And—this is important—she's not controlling, because she does not expect a deeper reaction from him in this first talk. In fact, she doesn't expect a personal reaction at all in this first talk. She knows he has to ride the train to find a personal reaction.

When she has expressed herself on the topic and asked two or three questions, she drops the subject. She does not keep talking about the topic hoping for some response. She does not press him for an immediate response. She goes silent for a few minutes or brings up another topic.

The Woman Shares in Two Categories

The woman will share from two categories in this first talk. The first category (which I covered in chapter 8) is: "He may or may not respond to my topic." It's completely up to him to ride the train and get back to the woman with a response. If her topic interests him and triggers something in him, he'll give her a response. If not, he won't.

The second category is: "I need a response to this topic." This topic is important to the woman, and she really needs him to respond. A response from him will mean a lot to her. These kinds of topics may make up 10 percent of all the topics the woman shares with the man.

The key for the woman is to tell the man directly and clearly when she is presenting an *I need a response* topic. Believe me, he will not realize it's in this important category unless she tells him. She can say to him something like, "Honey, I'm about to talk about something important to me. I need a response. Please get back to me on this topic."

The Man Rides the Train

The woman has stopped talking about her topic. The man has listened well and may have jotted down the topic using his pad or phone. He may also have jotted down the few questions the woman has asked him about the topic.

If it is a matter he wants to respond to, he'll ride the train and do some processing. Or if it is a topic about which she's made clear she needs a response, he'll ride the train. It may take several hours to several days for him to process and find an internal reaction to her topic.

While on the train, he'll dig down and find his reaction. He'll run through what she said, looking for his thoughts, opinions, and—most importantly—his emotions.

He'll try to see the situation from her point of view and consider the impact it has on her. He'll try to walk in her shoes and think about how he'd react if what she talked about happened to him. He'll think about events in his life that are similar in some way to what she talked about.

Your Second Conversation

When the man has found a personal response and is ready to deliver it, he finds the woman and restarts the conversation. This is the second conversation on her topic.

Chances are very good that he has taken at least a day, maybe two, to come up with a more personal, self-disclosing, intimate, vulnerable response. He will probably give his response in the second scheduled Couple Talk Time of the week.

In fact, giving his response in the second Couple Talk Time is exactly what I want him to do. My recommended four Couple Talk Times per week allow a couple to build, over time, an intimate conversation.

He shares his personal response and, by doing so, deepens the conversation on her topic. Being a woman, she responds right away to his response, and so the conversation gets even deeper. He listens to her response and . . . wait for it . . . starts another train trip to dig for more personal information.

More Train Trips, More Talks

The man and the woman have had two conversations on the same topic. They've gotten deeper, but they're not done yet.

The man will ride the train again in preparation for their third Couple Talk Time. At this third Talk Time, he'll get even deeper in his response. The woman will react to his train trip information with an even deeper, more personal response of her own.

Now they're getting somewhere in this ongoing conversation. Somewhere intimate. Somewhere meaningful. Somewhere revealing. Somewhere they usually don't get to because, up to now, they haven't used the train over four Couple Talk Times.

Will he ride the train again in preparation for their fourth Couple Talk Time of the week? Yes, he will. Will he bring her more intimate information in this final Talk Time of the week? Yes, he will. Will she respond to what he shares with her by sharing her own more personal information? Yes, she will. Will they reach a deep level of intimacy on the topic she brought up earlier that week? Yes, they will.

Conversational Teamwork

Can you see how it takes a week to build a more than superficial conversation? Using the train, it will be three or, even better, four talks on the same subject matter before the man really gets deep and expresses what's inside, and before the woman gets deep and expresses what's inside her by responding to him.

This is teamwork! You're working together to achieve a deep conversation. Each time the man returns from a train trip, he gets a little deeper. And the woman responds on a little deeper level as she hears and responds to him. They react to each other's responses!

Me, the Blonde, and Progressive Intimacy

The best talks Sandy and I have happen over the course of a week. We keep talking about the same two or three topics in our four Couple Talk Times. This way, with me riding the train and Sandy responding, we can touch all angles of an issue. We can truly get beneath the surface and get our two hearts and minds connected.

We spent years and years of our marriage killing conversations. Sandy would bring up a subject and talk about it. I had little to no response, so the conversation went nowhere. We killed it. Sandy would bring up another topic and talk about it. Because I knew nothing about the train and the process of progressive intimacy, I had nothing to say. So another conversation was killed. We were serial conversation killers! I'll bet you and your spouse are too!

Do what we learned how to do, and use the train over four Couple Talk Times. Extend your conversations! Talk about the same two or three areas of interest over the week. You'll be amazed at the emotional connection you will create.

Next, I want to discuss a very important issue in the life of most couples: how to get your spouse to talk about topics he (or she) doesn't want to talk about.

Can you relate to this? I know you can.

ASK YOURSELVES THESE QUESTIONS

1. How many times have the two of you killed a conversation before it could develop? What ways have you used to kill these conversations?

2. Have you ever talked about one topic three or four separate times over the course of a week? If so, did you reach a deeper level of understanding and intimacy by the end of the week?

3. Ladies, what will cause you to go beyond a limit of ten minutes in talking to your spouse about a subject?

4. Men, are you willing to schedule four Couple Talk Times each week? Are you willing to ride the train between Talk Times?

5. Think of at least one topic now that you can talk about, and use the train to think about, in your Couple Talk Times this next week.

PART FOUR

We Need to Talk about Difficult Topics!

CHAPTER 15

HE DOESN'T WANT TO TALK
ABOUT DIFFICULT TOPICS

HERE'S ONE OF THE WAYS A MAN drives his woman crazy. He will agree to talk with you about a topic, but then he never brings it up again. He doesn't want to have this conversation, so he "forgets" the topic.

Here's the weird and crazy-making part. He actually does forget the topic. I'm not kidding. It leaves his brain. He can sleep at night, talk with you about other things, and go on with life as if he never agreed to talk about this topic.

When you remind him of the topic, he will usually remember it at that point. But he'll say with a straight face, "I forgot." And he's telling the truth! You could hook him up to a lie detector and he'd pass!

Occasionally, I do this "I can't remember" routine with my Sandy. She'll say, "You're a clinical psychologist who teaches couples how to communicate. How can you forget?" I tell her, "I am a psychologist, but I'm also a guy."

I have a solution to Mr. No Memory that will keep you women sane and help the two of you talk about topics the man doesn't want to talk about.

Do I Have to Talk about It?

The train will help the Clam open up and talk with you about a variety of topics. But there are times when the Clam stubbornly stays shut and does not want to talk. When you bring up a subject that he does not want to talk about, he'll hop on the train, and *he won't come back.*

The problem is, these difficult issues need to be discussed for you two to stay close and in love. And certain tough decisions have to be made, together, to move your marriage and family forward.

The reactions your Clam will have to uncomfortable topics fall into two categories:

1. You've asked him to ride the train to think about a topic, and he is not returning with a response.

2. You want to discuss a difficult topic, and you know he will not want to talk about it.

I'll deal with the first category in this chapter and the second category in the next chapter.

He's Not Coming Back from a Train Trip

In one of your Couple Talk Times—or another time—you talked about something important to you, and you asked him to ride the train and come back with a response. This topic is in the 10 percent "I need a response" category.

He knows you want a response, but it doesn't look as though he's going to get back to you. It's been three days, and you've even had one Couple Talk Time since you asked him to ride the train. There is no train in sight.

You don't know why he's not giving you a response. You think maybe he simply forgot; it wouldn't be the first time something slipped his mind. It's also possible that, for some reason, he does not want to talk about this topic.

Your curiosity is aroused. You still want a response to your topic, but you also want to know why he is not getting back to you.

So what do you do?

Here's What You *Don't* Do

You already know what not to do. You know not to do the usual Crowbar behaviors because that will clam him up tight, and you'll never get his response to your topic.

- Don't remind him multiple times. It won't make any difference if you are sweet and kind each time you remind him; he'll feel pressured, and he will remain clammed up.

- Even if you remind him just once, don't use a frustrated, angry tone. He'll get frustrated and angry right back at you and never give you the response.

- Don't lecture him on how his lack of response to your topic makes you feel. Though you are speaking the truth, Clams do not appreciate being lectured. He'll feel controlled and demeaned, and you kiss good-bye any hope of a response.

- Don't go silent and pouty. He's a man, so he'll have no idea that you're upset because he has not responded to your topic. He just knows you're upset, and he'll do what most men do when their women are upset: He will avoid you until you're not upset.

Here's what I want you to do when he is not returning from a train trip about a subject that is important to you. I want you to follow a creative, out-of-the-box (if I do say so myself) approach. My recommendation may be one of the most brilliant communication strategies ever devised for couples. Please be sitting down when you read my strategy.

The Hostage Negotiator

Collect all his underwear—every pair except the ones he's wearing—and hide it all. When he comes to you and asks where his underwear is, you say, with a straight face:

> "This is a hostage situation. I am in contact with your
> missing underwear. Not close contact for obvious reasons, but
> I know where it is. When you give me a response to that issue
> I brought up three days ago (remind him of it), you will get
> your underwear back."

Okay, I'm kidding again. This underwear operation may be tempting, but it won't work. Most men would simply continue wearing their one pair of underwear or (I know this is repulsive to you) not wear any at all.

One Reminder

Here's what I want you to do in this "no response from your man to something important to you" situation. Go to him and give him one low-key reminder. Any more reminders and he'll see you as a nag, he'll feel pressure, and he will never respond.

So you are allowed one reminder. This is a calm, reasonable, amiable, adult-to-adult reminder. You're not upset or angry. Yet. Say to the Clam:

> "Remember the issue (tell him what it is) I talked about in our
> last Couple Talk Time? When you're ready, I need to hear your
> response. If it's hard for you to discuss, that's okay. When you
> come back, we can talk about that, too."

That's it. Give the reminder and walk away. The conversational ball is in his court. You won't bring it up again.

He knows this issue is important to you, because you told him this the first time you asked him to ride the train and get back to you. Now, your reminder reinforces the fact that you want a response.

You've also given him permission to talk about why the topic is hard for him to discuss. That, in itself, could be an interesting part of the conversation when he returns.

He Still Won't Talk about It!

If he refuses to return with a response, now you're angry, and you have every right to be angry. He has insulted and disrespected you. Go to him one last time on this matter, and say words like these:

> "You have chosen to not give me a response regarding that topic you know is important to me. I'm angry and frustrated. I don't ask you to ride the train to think about many issues. I need to get my feelings out so I can let this go and we can move on."

When you've made your statement, walk away. You will never bring up that topic again.

Mr. Clam, this is actually your last chance to give this woman you profess to love a response to her important topic. Wait a few minutes, then go after her and apologize for ignoring her important request. Let her vent her feelings about your lack of response. Listen and reflect, and give her multiple, heartfelt, sincere "I'm sorrys."

She'll be hard on you, but take it with grace and kindness and guts. It's your own fault for stiffing her and hurting her. Then, when she's convinced you are genuinely sorry, give her a response on the topic that concerns her. She still wants to hear what you have to say about it, and she wants to continue the conversation.

Crowbars, in the next chapter, I'm going to help you motivate your Clam to talk about difficult, sensitive topics you know he does not want to talk about.

ASK YOURSELVES THESE QUESTIONS

1. Mrs. Crowbar, what type of topics do you really, really want your Clam to ride the train to think about and then give you a response?

2. Mr. Clam, what type of topics do you really, really *not* want to ride the train to think about and then come up with a response? Why don't you want to talk about these topics?

3. Mrs. Crowbar, what do you usually do when he does not get back to you on a topic important to you?

4. Mr. Clam, how many pairs of underwear do you own? (Kidding.)

5. Mrs. Crowbar, what will be difficult about giving him only one low-key reminder?

6. Mr. Clam, do you think this one reminder strategy will work for you? If the topic is a difficult one for you, will you be able to tell her why?

CHAPTER 16

HOW TO TALK ABOUT DIFFICULT TOPICS

Here's another classic Clam-Crowbar discussion I've had with hundreds of couples in therapy.

> **Wife (Crowbar):** Dr. Clarke, I can't get my husband to talk about difficult, sensitive topics. As soon as I bring up a topic that he thinks will be tough to deal with, he shuts down. He walks away. He refuses to have the conversation. It's so frustrating!

> **Me (psychologist and Clam):** Bob, why do you have this reaction? (I know why, but I have to ask anyway.)

> **Husband (Clam):** Doc, these types of conversations never go well. And I mean never. They always end up in a fight and we both say hurtful things. Rather than doing more damage, I figure it's better to not even try to have the discussion.

Me: Look, you have to have these conversations on difficult, sensitive, awkward topics. If you don't, you can't fix the issues and you'll kill your intimacy. It's how you have these conversations that makes all the difference. I can show you how.

I Don't Want to Talk about It

In the second "How can I get him to respond" scenario, you want to discuss a topic you know he does not want to talk about.

Your track record in this department is not good. The sad truth is, your success rate is just about zero. You have tried many times in the past to bring up tough issues, and he has resisted all your attempts to have a reasonable dialogue about a difficult subject.

Being a Clam, he has:

- gotten defensive immediately

- gotten angry quickly

- shut down in a hurry

- ignored you right away

Sometimes he has agreed to talk about "it"—but "later." Of course, "later" never comes. He conveniently forgets or refuses to talk about it if you bring it up again.

You're officially tired of hitting the brick wall (or facing the closed clamshell) and not being able to discuss difficult, awkward, but important topics with him.

What do you do? Follow these four steps, and you'll significantly improve your chances of him talking with you about difficult topics.

Step One: Schedule the First Meeting

Go to your Clam and schedule a meeting for just the two of you, in private, of course, in which you will make a one-way presentation on a difficult subject. Make it clear that you will be the only one talking at this meeting. Let him know that all you want him to do is listen to you and understand what you're saying.

In scheduling this meeting, say something like:

"Honey, I have something important I want to tell you about. It is a difficult subject, and it's hard to bring it up. Let's have the meeting at the kitchen table two days from now. How about Thursday evening at eight? At this meeting, I'll talk about the topic, and I don't want you to respond. All I want you to do is listen to me and understand what I'm saying."

When you give him some time before the meeting, he is able to prepare mentally and feel more in control. Springing a tough issue on a Clam never goes well. If you let him know it will be a tough issue, he won't be surprised.

Do not tell him what the topic is. If you do, he'll rapidly go into defensive maneuvers.

Knowing he will not be expected to respond at this meeting lowers the level of pressure for him. He will have time to process what you say, and that's exactly what he needs. And, also important, you can make a full presentation on the topic without activating his usual quick-on-the-trigger defensive reactions.

Bypassing his typical negative reactions to a sensitive topic gets you into the conversation. At least you have created the opportunity for a dialogue to occur.

If you allow him to respond in a huffy, critical, or defensive manner right away, the conversation is over. No more discussion will happen.

Choosing a neutral place in your home for a difficult conversation is also a key to success. Do not use the warm, fuzzy place you hold your Couple Talk Times. That place is for only positive, uplifting conversations.

Use a room or space in your home that doesn't mean much to you. The kitchen table. An office. A spare bedroom. A living room you never use. The laundry room. Limiting your hard conversations to one neutral place gives you control and structure. You will have virtually all your tough talks in this one place.

Negotiate the time of this first meeting with him. Don't tell him when it will be, because he'll feel as if he's being called to the principal's office. If he has input into when, he's already part of the process, and that's a good thing.

Step Two: Give Your One-Way Presentation

At this first meeting, you thank him for being there and repeat that you'll talk and all you want is for him to listen.

Give him your presentation in ten minutes or less, unless it's a complicated issue that requires more time. If he tries to interrupt, say, "Honey, I don't want a response. Just listen."

When you are done, tell him:

"Thanks for listening. I know that wasn't easy. Honey, I ask you to take a day or two to process what I've said. Think about it and pray about it. When you're ready, let me know, and we'll meet back here so I can hear your response. If you need more than two days to process and respond, that's okay. Take the time you need, and let me know when you're ready. When we meet, I will just listen to what you say. I will not give a response at this meeting. I'll just work to understand your point of view, your thoughts, and your feelings."

You're giving him time to ride the train and do his processing. This will help him get past his knee-jerk defensiveness and actually consider what you've said to him. You're allowing him to decide when he'll give his response, so he will not feel controlled or pressured.

You're putting his mind at ease by telling him you won't give a response right after he shares his *position* on the issue. This will help him share more freely and openly.

Step Three: He Rides the Train and Gives His Response

He sets up the second meeting and, in your difficult conversation place, gives his response to your topic. You listen and reflect what he says and what he tells you are his feelings. You do not disagree, you do not interrupt, you do not seek to correct him. You do not make any response at all in this meeting.

If you give him the respect of letting him talk and you communicate understanding of what he's saying and feeling, it is very likely that he'll be willing to continue talking about this topic.

At the end of this second meeting, do two things: First, make sure he believes you fully understand his position on the issue. Ask him, "Honey, do you believe I get what you are saying? Do you think I fully understand your position and feelings about this?"

If he says yes, you're good to go. If he says no, ask him what he thinks you don't get. Ask him to talk more about the topic in the area or areas he thinks you don't understand. Keep reflecting until he says he thinks you get it.

Second, tell him:

"Sweetheart, we have each given our positions on this topic. Let's take a few days to process what we've shared. Then let's meet again in this place to have a dialogue about the topic and what decisions we need to make. I'll let you know when I'm ready to talk, and you tell me when you're ready."

At this point in the process, you have avoided the premature shutdown of the difficult conversation. You have achieved understanding of your two positions. Most of the emotions connected to the tough topic have been expressed and, therefore, reduced in intensity.

You are ready for the final step, a step you may never have reached before in dealing with a difficult topic.

Step Four: Two-Way Dialogue about the Topic

In this final step, you meet in your conflict/difficult conversation place and talk back and forth about the topic. You can have a reasonable, adult dialogue now because of the previous three steps.

You can talk about the different aspects of the issue, share more information and opinions and feelings if needed, and make a good decision. You may have a number of conversations in this step before you reach a conclusion, and that's okay. You're talking about it, and you'll be able to figure it out—together.

Do It One-Way, and Do It Slowly

As you have probably realized, these four steps are an industrial strength version of the one-way communication I covered in chapter 8. And the train technique from chapter 13 is also utilized.

With difficult topics, never wing it. Don't freelance. Deal with these topics slowly and by using my four steps. With conflict, speed kills. Take your time, follow the rules, and you can—as a team—talk through any issue.

The Secret to Lasting Intimacy

All the chapters to this point are designed to create emotional intimacy in your relationship. By adjusting to your Clam-Crowbar differences, you can communicate on a deep, personal, soul-satisfying level.

As critically important as your emotional connection is, it is not enough to produce a powerful, lasting intimacy. There is another area of intimacy that, together with your emotional connection, will give you a special closeness that will last a lifetime.

This second area you have to experience is spiritual intimacy. In the next six chapters, I will teach you how to spiritually bond.

ASK YOURSELVES THESE QUESTIONS

1. Mr. Clam, what topics do you not want to discuss with your Crowbar? Why? When she brings up these difficult, sensitive subjects, how do you respond? How, specifically, do you avoid having that conversation?

2. Does it make sense to you, Clam, that my four-step process can get you past your initial resistance and defensiveness and into the conversation?

3. Mrs. Crowbar, tell him why it is so important to you to occasionally have these talks about difficult issues.

4. Tell each other what you think will happen to your relationship if you continue to not have these "difficult topic" conversations.

5. Are you both willing to try my four-step process? If so, pick a topic that at present is causing one or both of you concern, and practice talking about it using my four steps.

PART FIVE

We Need to Spiritually Bond!

CHAPTER 17

YOU WANT THE GOLD, DON'T YOU?

I LOVE WATCHING THE OLYMPICS. Hundreds of elite, world-class athletes coming together in one place for one incredible competition.

Every athlete has made many sacrifices to reach the Olympic Games. Years and years of preparation. Time away from families. Careers put on hold. Huge amounts of money for training, coaches, transportation, housing, food, and myriad other necessary expenses.

And all for what? To show up at this magnificent competition and be able to say, "I was there." That's it. Participation is the goal. These athletes don't care if they win or lose. Just being at the Olympics and enjoying the spectacle, making new friends, and representing their country is more than enough reward.

You know this isn't even close to the truth. Olympic athletes sacrifice, train, and compete to *win*. The gold medal is their only objective. The bronze medal is fine. The silver medal is good. But these single-minded athletes desperately want the gold.

Go for the Gold in Your Relationship

You now know how to achieve emotional intimacy. By following my strategies, you will develop revealing, in-depth conversations. And that's important! I wouldn't have spent sixteen chapters on it if it wasn't essential to the success of your relationship.

At this point, you can definitely get to the bronze medal level in the "relationship intimacy" event. You can probably even earn the silver medal. That's pretty impressive and a better relationship than most couples will ever enjoy.

As valuable and satisfying as those medals are, are you satisfied with bronze or silver? I hope not! What if I told you that you can get the gold medal? You'd want it, wouldn't you? Of course you would.

You can earn the gold medal, relationally speaking, by learning how to be *spiritually intimate* as a couple. Your spiritual bond, added to your emotional bond, will give you the closest, strongest relationship possible between a man and a woman.

In the next five chapters, I'm going to show you how to spiritually bond.

God's Definition of Male-Female Intimacy

Genesis 2:24 contains the first message in the Bible about male-female intimacy: "Therefore a man shall leave his father and his mother and hold fast to his wife, and they shall become *one flesh*" (italics added).

These two words, "one flesh," are God's definition of heterosexual intimacy. Since it is God's definition, it must be *the* best one!

What is "one flesh"? One flesh is a complete coming together of a husband and a wife in three areas:

physically . . . two bodies
emotionally . . . two minds
spiritually . . . two souls

God says you have true, complete intimacy only when you are bonded in all three areas.

Let me ask you two vital questions: Which of these three areas is the most important in a relationship? Which area of intimacy is the best foundation for a relationship?

Physical Intimacy

Can you base a relationship on physical or sexual intimacy? Yes, you can. Is it a good idea? No, it is not.

My thirty years of working with couples shows that a relationship based on the physical will last six months to a year and a half. No longer. Sexual attraction alone is not enough to sustain a relationship. It will not create a permanent, meaningful bond.

Let's face it, when you've seen the same naked body twenty times, fifty times, one hundred and twenty-two times, not much is going to change. I mean, there is that body, looking pretty much exactly as it did the last time. You cannot, and you will not, continue to draw intimacy from only that body.

To attempt to build a permanent, truly satisfying relationship mainly on physical attraction has a devastating effect on a relationship. Because of the physical ecstasy of this part of a relationship, the other areas may not be cultivated and partners do not grow in them. This is a disaster for their marriage and for their lives.

Man and woman are not just physical beings. They are emotional, intellectual, and spiritual beings.

Many of my clients could testify that sex alone isn't enough to sustain a relationship. They might tell me, "Dr. Clarke, I've had several relationships based strictly on sex, and they didn't last."

I'd reply, "No, of course they didn't. As powerful as sex is, physical intimacy was never designed by God to carry a relationship fifty to sixty or more years." There's a reason sex outside of marriage isn't God's plan.

Emotional Intimacy

Can you base a relationship on emotional intimacy? Yes, you can. Is this a good idea? No, it is not.

In my clinical experience, a relationship based on emotional intimacy will last four to seven years. Now, that's better than six to eighteen months, but it still isn't very long.

Even if you work hard at understanding your differences and follow my proven communication strategies, the emotional intimacy you create will not last past seven years. Truthfully, you'll be lucky to reach seven years.

Many of my clients could also testify that emotional intimacy alone isn't enough to sustain a relationship. They might tell me, "Dr. Clarke, in my previous marriage, we loved each other, and we worked hard on communication. But we lost our love."

I'd reply, "I'm sorry, but of course you did. As significant as emotional intimacy is, it was never designed by God to carry a relationship for the duration of the couple's lives."

Spiritual Intimacy

Can you base a relationship on spiritual intimacy? Yes, you can. Is this a good idea? Because this is your last choice, you know the answer: Yes, it is!

A relationship based on spiritual intimacy will last a lifetime, for as long as you both shall live. These are strong words, but they're true.

The spiritual is the most important part of us. We are spiritual beings above all else. The spiritual, therefore, must also be the most important part of our relationships with the opposite sex.

The most important part of my love for Sandy comes from God and the connection we share in Him. On my own, in human strength only, I can't love Sandy deeply or consistently. Not just because it's so hard to live with a woman, though that's true! But because I need God's help to truly love her with an Ephesians 5:25 love: "Love your wives, as Christ loved the church and gave himself up for her."

Of course, this goes both ways. Without hesitation, Sandy would tell you that she needs God's help to truly love me.

The Secret to Genuine, Lasting Intimacy

The secret is becoming one flesh spiritually. I call this *spiritual bonding*. Here's what spiritual bonding is: *consistently placing God at the very center of your relationship and growing ever closer to Him as a couple.*

It is two souls coming together in the pursuit of God.

Spiritual Bonding Creates Genuine Intimacy

When you bond spiritually, God gives you the best kind of intimacy. The deepest kind, literally God-empowered. Strictly by itself, coming together as a couple spiritually produces a passion and an energy unmatched in human experience.

When you connect spiritually in the presence of God, the walls between you as a man and a woman come down. God brings them down. And when God brings your walls down, they're all the way down.

You are two persons, two souls, coming together:

- to know God better

- to worship God

- to love God

Spiritual Bonding Feeds Your Emotional Intimacy

While your spiritual intimacy is the most important "one flesh" area, your emotional intimacy is also vital to a successful relationship. I made this clear at the beginning of this chapter.

You have learned how to connect emotionally, but you can't sustain that connection without God's ongoing power in your relationship.

As you build your spiritual bond, God will help you understand and work with your Clam-Crowbar differences. God will help you share openly and honestly. God will help you continue to communicate on deeper levels.

Spiritual Bonding Feeds Your Physical Intimacy

Physical chemistry is essential to a love relationship. In fact, it's how every romantic relationship begins.

We are attracted to a member of the opposite sex first by that person's body. You don't walk up and say, "Hey, I was standing over there and I noticed you, and I have to tell you I really like your body." This approach wouldn't be a good idea. The police might be called.

But physical chemistry is what happens in a first meeting, and that's okay. It's normal. It's how God made us!

I will never forget seeing Sandy for the first time. My roommate, Dave Brown, and I were standing in front of the gym at Point Loma College in San Diego, California. He said, "Dave, there's Sandy Martin, the girl from my hometown that I was telling you about."

I turned and saw Sandy. I didn't think, "Wow, what a great mind she must have!" At nineteen, I could have cared less about her mind. I thought, "Whoa, she is beautiful!" And—of course—when she saw me she was thinking the same thing about me. When I use that line in my marriage seminars, I always get a big laugh. I can't imagine why they would laugh.

Your relationship begins with physical attraction, and in God's plan, physical intimacy remains an integral part of your life together. God wants you to enjoy making love throughout your marriage! He dedicated an entire book of the Bible, Song of Solomon, to romance, sensuality, and sex. The apostle Paul instructs husbands and wives not to neglect having sexual relations (see 1 Corinthians 7:5).

How do you keep your physical attraction and sex life vibrant? By keeping God at the center of your marriage. After eighteen months, you need spiritual bonding to maintain your physical passion and enjoy a healthy, growing sexual relationship.

Spiritual Bonding Is the Source of All Love

You have to have emotional and physical intimacy to have a great marriage. And there are specific strategies you can follow as a couple to improve these areas. But the main continuing source of both emotional and physical intimacy is *spiritual* bonding.

Would God make us spiritual beings, then allow us to ignore the spiritual part of the marriage relationship and still have complete satisfaction and intimacy? No. No, He would not.

Does it make sense that if you put God at the center of your relationship, He will bless and energize every other area? That's exactly what He will do!

God has done this for Sandy and me as well as countless clients in my therapy practice, and He'll do it for you and your partner.

I've told you how critical spiritual bonding is for your relationship. Next, I'm going to tell you how to achieve it.

ASK YOURSELVES THESE QUESTIONS

1. Have you had relationships that were strictly physical? How long did they last? Do you know others who had relationships based purely on the physical? If so, how long did those relationships last?

2. Have you had relationships based on emotional intimacy? How long did they last? Do you know others whose relationships were based on their emotional closeness? How long did they last?

3. Have you ever heard—from a parent, a pastor, a friend, a book, or a video—about *spiritual bonding* in marriage?

4. Have you known any couples who have bonded *spiritually*? If so, what are these marriages like in terms of intimacy and longevity?

CHAPTER 18

IT'S ALL ABOUT JESUS

You walk into a classroom on the first day of class. You have signed up for this course and feel prepared to take it. Just before the class begins, the teacher walks over to you and says, "I'm sorry, but you cannot take this course. My records indicate that you have not taken the prerequisite."

It's embarrassing and awkward, but you have to leave the class and drop the course. You sign up for the prerequisite class. When you complete it, then—and only then—can you move on and take the next course.

All schools of higher education—high school and up—have a progressive system of courses. There are certain foundational courses you must take called prerequisites before you can take more advanced courses. Spanish 101 comes before Spanish 102. Algebra 101 comes before Algebra 102.

The same applies to spiritual bonding. Before you can begin the process of putting God at the center of your relationship, there are two prerequisites you must meet. These two actions must come first.

Prerequisite Number One: Each Person Must Be a Christian

There's a lot of confusion these days about what makes one a Christian. Many say they are Christians when they are not.

Becoming a Christian is all about Jesus.

There is one God, and He is the God of the Bible. There is one way to establish a relationship with God, and that is through His Son, Jesus Christ.

Here is Jesus Christ, in His own words: "I am the way, and the truth, and the life. No one comes to the Father except through me" (John 14:6).

A Christian is someone who has a personal relationship with God through Jesus. God sent Jesus to die for your sins—all the things you've done wrong—to provide forgiveness so that you can have a relationship with God: "For God so loved the world, that he gave his only Son, that whoever believes in him should not perish but have eternal life" (John 3:16).

This is what you must believe to become a Christian: "For I delivered to you as of first importance what I also received: that Christ died for our sins in accordance with the Scriptures, that he was buried, that he was raised on the third day in accordance with the Scriptures" (1 Corinthians 15:3-4).

When you believe these three truths—Jesus died for your sins, He was buried, He rose from the dead—and ask Jesus to be *your* Savior, you become a Christian. You have a personal relationship with God through His Son, Jesus. You are forgiven!

You now have the power to improve your personal life. You have the ability to spiritually bond with your partner. And best of all, you're going to heaven when you die.

You Can Become a Christian—Right Now

If you are not a Christian yet, I urge you to become one. You can begin your relationship with God through Jesus right now by expressing your feelings and your decision by the words in this brief prayer. But know that believing, or placing your faith in Christ, is not only cognitive assent, or just agreeing with certain assertions. It's about the intent of your heart:

Dear God,
I know I am a sinner. I've made many mistakes and sinned in my life. I realize my sin separates me from You, a holy God. I believe that Your Son, Jesus Christ, died for my sins, was buried, and rose from the dead. I place my trust in Him as my Savior. I give my life to You now.

If you prayed this prayer of belief, I am thrilled for you. And God is thrilled.

But if you're not ready to commit your life to Christ, here's what I want you to do: First, read Lee Strobel's book *The Case for Christ,* or watch a DVD version. Lee presents a compelling argument for who Jesus Christ is and how He will change your life and your eternity. After watching or reading, discuss the book or DVD with your partner.

Second, read the Gospel of John. This book of the Bible will introduce you to Jesus in a personal and powerful way. After reading it, discuss it with your partner.

Third, attend a local church with your partner for at least one month. After that month, meet alone with the pastor to discuss *The Case for Christ* and the Gospel of John. Get the pastor's input on Jesus.

These three steps will allow you to explore the claims of Jesus Christ and will give you the opportunity to make a decision about Him. The most important decision in all of life is to begin a relationship with Jesus!

Here's an important truth you need to understand: *To spiritually bond, both partners must be spiritually alive.* "You were dead in the trespasses and sins. . . . But God, being rich in mercy, because of the great love with which he loved us, even when we were dead in our trespasses, made us alive together with Christ—by grace you have been saved" (Ephesians 2:1, 4-5).

If one partner is not a Christian and therefore spiritually dead, there can be no spiritual bonding.

"What If My Partner Is Not a Christian?"

Good question. Here's my answer: If you're dating a nonbeliever, break up. This will be a very difficult and painful action, but it is the right thing to do.

I'm trying to spare you the ongoing grief, agony, and disappointment you will experience if you marry a person who is not a Christian. He or she could be a wonderful person whom you really love. But you cannot have spiritual intimacy with someone who doesn't know Jesus!

If you can't spiritually bond, you will never—I repeat, never—have a great marriage. You will never be "one flesh." You will never experience the full measure of intimacy—spiritual, emotional, physical—that God designed you to experience.

"What If My Spouse Is Not a Christian?"

Another good question. This is a very different scenario. Your marriage is sacred to God, so I will never recommend divorce. I've never recommended divorce in thirty years of counseling couples, and I never will.

If you are in this situation, here's what I want you to do: Follow my strategy in chapter 22 for as long as it takes. Build a solid support system, stay very close to God, be the best spouse you can be, and keep working my strategy.

Prerequisite Number Two: Each Person Must Be Growing Spiritually

To know God through Jesus Christ is crucially important. To grow in your relationship with God is equally important. A big part of the spiritual bond is sharing the personal growth you each experience. You can't share what you don't have.

If one partner is not growing spiritually, automatically the couple's spiritual bond stagnates and dies. The no-spiritual-growth partner is not close to God, has nothing to share about his or her daily fellowship with God, and cannot connect spiritually with the other partner.

A Daily Individual Quiet Time with God

To grow in your relationship with God the Father, you must spend regular time with Him. Every day, invest fifteen minutes or more with God. I've already told you that virtually all of your emotional intimacy will occur in your four Couple Talk Times each week. Well, virtually all of your personal spiritual intimacy will occur in your daily individual times with God.

Your quiet time with God can be at any time of the day. In a private, no-distractions-allowed, quiet (hence the term "quiet time") place, meet with God. When you meet with God your Father, Jesus your Savior and the Holy Spirit will be there too.

I want you to do three things in each quiet time.

First, begin by reading a daily devotion. This is a brief spiritual message, usually tied to a Bible passage, that helps you focus on God and spiritual things. It acts like a spiritual cup of coffee. It gets your soul warmed up. There are many excellent daily devotionals, both online and in hold-in-your-hands book form. Check with your pastor or Focus on the Family to find one.

Second, pray. Praying is simply talking with God. I say "with" because you talk to God, and God "speaks" to you through what He has given us—the Bible. He also speaks when you sit in silence, listen, and meditate on His Word and who He is. Open up and share everything with Him: what's going on in your life, the good things He's given you, your struggles and anxieties, your fears, failures, sins, spiritual insights, spiritual doubts . . . Always take time to worship and adore Him for who He is. Never,

ever forget to thank Him for all He has done. End with your requests for Him to meet your needs and the needs of others.

Finally, read the Bible. The Bible is, quite literally, God's Word. When you read Scripture, God is talking to you: comforting, admonishing, convicting, encouraging, and teaching you. Read a short passage, a verse or several verses, and meditate on this for a few minutes. Consider how you can apply what you read to your life that very day.

You and your partner will grow spiritually at different rates. That's okay, as long as you're both growing.

"What If My Partner Is Not Growing Spiritually?"

Your dating partner is a Christian but is not going anywhere spiritually. It's been a while since your partner has worked on his or her spiritual life. Follow my six-month strategy I explain in chapter 22. If your partner has not responded at the end of the six months, break up.

"What If My Spouse Is Not Growing Spiritually?"

You believe your spouse is a Christian who has truly believed in Jesus as his or her Savior, but you see zero spiritual signs of growth. Again, follow my six-month strategy described in chapter 22. If you see no response, you won't think of divorce. You will continue my strategy until your spouse decides to grow spiritually, or until the day when one of you dies and your marriage ends.

You know the two prerequisites: Each person must be a Christian, and each person must be growing spiritually. Now I'm going to show you how to spiritually bond.

ASK YOURSELVES THESE QUESTIONS

1. Do you have a personal relationship with God that comes from trusting in Christ for your salvation? If you do not, do you want this relationship? Are you ready to begin this relationship now?

2. What is keeping you from beginning this relationship with God? Are you willing to read Lee Strobel's book *The Case for Christ*, read the Gospel of John, attend a local church for one month, and talk to the pastor?

3. Are you growing spiritually? How would you describe your relationship with God right now?

4. If you are not growing spiritually, not growing closer to God, why not? What has happened to stop your spiritual growth? Ask your spouse to consider this question as he or she observes your life.

5. Are you willing to have a daily, individual quiet time with God in which you read a devotional, pray, and read and meditate on a Bible passage? What would keep you from these spiritual growth practices?

CHAPTER 19

PRAYING AS A COUPLE

SANDY AND I HAD BEEN MARRIED fifteen years. Life wasn't just busy. It was barely controlled chaos. Emily was twelve, Leeann was ten, Nancy was seven, and William was three. I think you are starting to get the picture.

I was a clinical psychologist in private practice, and Sandy was a mom and a homemaker. Believe me, she had the tougher job!

Our lives were a constant, crazy whirl of activity: getting the kids to school, picking them up after school, homework, the dreaded science projects, school activities, piano practice at home, birthday parties, sleepovers, playing in the yard and the pool, church services, church activities, time with our friends and their kids, flying to California and Colorado to be with family . . .

Life was good. Hectic, but good. And our marriage was good. But for the Blonde and me, a good marriage wasn't good enough. We were slipping in the areas of communication, quality time for the two of us, and physical intimacy.

We were not at a crisis point, but we decided to take action to avoid real problems down the road. We'd seen too many couples—friends, family, neighbors, therapy clients—drift apart and get divorced, or stay together in miserable, joyless marriages.

That was not going to happen to us!

So we did something revolutionary. Something we had never done before. Something no one had ever recommended to us. We started to pray together, just the two of us, on a regular basis.

Up to this point, we had prayed before meals. We had prayed at church. We had prayed when in a crisis. Sometimes we prayed briefly in bed just before going to sleep.

But we had never prayed in a regular, intentional, and deeper way. We were already having four Couple Talk Times each week. These Talk Times were enriching our emotional intimacy, but they were not getting us to a deeper level.

We were stuck in a "good" marriage.

We chose to add five minutes of prayer to each Couple Talk Time. We figured it couldn't hurt. The way it turned out, we had no idea how much it was going to help us!

Twenty minutes of prayer took our marriage from good to great. I'm not exaggerating. We developed—actually, God developed—a sweet, deep, and powerful closeness we had never come near to experiencing in our relationship.

We continue to pray in our Couple Talk Times, and it continues to keep us close—to God and to each other.

I don't write about something or recommend it to my clients until Sandy and I have tried it. That way, I know if it works. *And prayer works.*

Let me show you how to pray together.

Pray in Your Four Couple Talk Times

Add five minutes of prayer to every Couple Talk Time. It could be in the beginning, in the middle, or at the end of a Talk Time. Find out which spot works best for you.

Sandy and I usually begin our Talk Times with our five minutes of prayer. The prayer warms us up and gets us to a deeper level more quickly. When we start talking, our conversation is more open and more intimate.

Prayer also gives us some great topics of conversation. We have just prayed about the people and issues most important to us. So when we open our eyes and start talking, we'll talk about these same topics we just prayed about.

When You Pray, Hold Hands

This seems like a small thing, but it is a significant action. Holding hands connects you in a warm and loving way. It is a beautiful picture of unity, and it reminds you that you are becoming one flesh. It has a way of lowering defenses and helping you both to be open and vulnerable.

Pray Out Loud

If you are the Clam in your relationship, right now you're thinking, *Oh, no! I have to pray out loud? That is going to be really hard for me.* No worries. Praying out loud will be difficult, but I'm going to ease you into it.

It is perfectly fine—and very common—for the Clam to pray silently for the first few weeks. Maybe the first month. The Crowbar will pray out loud and, when finished, will squeeze the Clam's hand. The Clam will then pray silently and, when done, squeeze the Crowbar's hand.

Eventually the Clam will feel comfortable enough to begin to pray out loud. The Clam's initial out-loud prayers will probably be brief.

"Dear God, thank You for my marriage and my kids. Please bless us."
Or "Father, help us make the right decision as we look for a new home.
Amen."

As both partners begin to pray aloud, true spiritual bonding will
occur. When you know what your partner is saying to God, you know
his or her spiritual condition. You have a window into your partner's
personal relationship with God. That is big-time spiritual intimacy!

Take Turns in Praying

The best way to begin is to pray for things you have agreed on in advance.
Bring up prayer concerns—children, relatives, friends, health issues, your
church's ministries, job problems, finances—and develop a list. Decide
what to pray for, divide the list between you, and pray, one partner at a
time, for several minutes. First one prays, and then the other prays, until
you have prayed through your list of praises and requests.

I want you to continue to pray in this way for several months. As you
go along, both of you will find it easier to be more open and personal
in your prayers. You will be sharing more details about your individual
lives, things you're concerned about—that hang heavy on your heart,
things you are thankful for, things God is teaching you, your fears,
stresses, spiritual doubts . . .

In time, you may move in your prayers from reporting details to
expressing your emotions about the details. You'll go from the general
to the specific, from the superficial to the deep.

For example, a man might mention in his prayer that he's having a
problem at work. He just keeps it general, so his wife has no idea what's
really happening. She's dying to ask him twenty questions about what
the problem is, but she's learned that approach never works.

She knows that it was hard for him even to admit the problem at
all, so she does not use her crowbar. She holds off and lets him ride the
train. In this case, it's a "spiritual" train.

A few weeks later—that's right, a few weeks—he describes in more detail his work situation. He tells God (and his wife, who of course is also listening) that his supervisor is badgering him, and he asks the Lord for patience and strength to deal with this person.

A week later, the husband might finally feel comfortable enough to open up in prayer and share his feelings of frustration, anger, and help-lessness about his ongoing work situation.

After this prayer, they have a good talk about his problem at work.

You can see how the Clam is able to get deeper and deeper in his prayers about an important personal issue. The Crowbar does not put any pressure on her Clam to get deeper faster. After he prays, she prays using supportive and encouraging words. In her prayers, she comments only on what he has shared.

- "God, please help Bob with this problem at work, whatever it is."

- "God, I also ask that You give Bob the patience and strength to deal successfully with his supervisor."

- "Father, Bob is really struggling with this work issue. It is very painful to him. Give him what he needs to get through it."

It is in his prayers, and in her prayers in response, that this man is encouraged and motivated to share more and more on a personal level about his work problem. God uses their prayers to help the man open up and be honest and vulnerable. Now they can have a series of deeper, more detailed conversations about his work crisis.

Pray Conversationally

After a number of months—probably five or six at least—you'll be able to pray conversationally. This is a deeper level, and it takes time to get there. Hand in hand, with your eyes closed, you take turns talking to

God. You still have a basic list of prayer items, but you don't each pray for a certain predetermined number of them. You just start and then go back and forth. The man prays a few sentences, the woman prays a few sentences, and they keep repeating this, just as in an ordinary conversation. The only difference is that you're aware that God is also present. It's not a two-way conversation; it's a three-way conversation.

Conversational prayer is free-flowing, spontaneous, and personal. You don't worry about what specific things are on your list at this point. You mention anything and everything that comes to mind. You respond to each other. You may repeat what your partner prays. You may add to what your partner prays. Something your spouse prays may trigger something in your mind, and you will pray about that. You don't know where you are going in your prayers, and that's fine. That's the idea. You just let it happen.

When you pray conversationally, you allow the Holy Spirit much more room to maneuver and influence what's happening. You're open to His guidance and direction. He could take you anywhere. It is up to Him. The exciting thing is that it is not you who are praying but God, giving you the words through the Holy Spirit.

As the apostle Paul says in Romans 8:26, "Likewise the Spirit helps us in our weakness. For we do not know what to pray for as we ought, but the Spirit himself intercedes for us with groanings too deep for words." Have you ever wondered—as I have—what this verse really means? You will find out in conversational prayer. There's no experience quite like the Spirit moving in your prayer time.

At first you may pray conversationally about safe topics. As you get the hang of it, you'll pray about personal things—needs, worries, pain, joys, victories. Then you'll pray about your relationship with one another in an honest and vulnerable way. One spouse will mention a need, and the other spouse will pray for God's help to meet that need. You can communicate on the deepest possible level because you have the Holy Spirit Himself moving between you and giving you the words to say.

To give you a glimpse of what conversational prayer is like, I've included a brief excerpt from one couple's prayer time:

Wife: Dear Father, I'm worried about Doug. His drug and alcohol problems are out of control. We love his parents and want to help.

Husband: Father, I'm worried about Doug too. We've known him for years. We don't want him to ruin his life. Give his parents wisdom and strength. And move Doug to decide to get into rehab.

Wife: I agree with what Bob said. And Father, help us to be strong and close in our marriage. We need to stay close and united to be good parents to our kids.

Husband: Betty's right, Father. We need to be close as a couple, but lately we haven't been. I'm too busy at work, preoccupied with issues there. I need to be home more with Betty and the kids.

Wife: We do need to get back on track as a couple, Father. I'm too focused on church and my role at the kids' school. Help me to know where to cut back.

Husband: Father, hearing Betty pray makes me realize that we're just too busy. We do need to back off some things. I know I've skipped quite a few quiet times with You in the last two weeks.

Wife: Please, Lord, give Bob wisdom about how to handle his
schedule and all its demands. We all need him to be our
leader and . . .

Do you see how it works? Bob and Betty start out praying for their
friends' son, move to their marriage, and then move to their personal
and spiritual lives. With the Holy Spirit's guidance, this conversational
prayer could go any number of places. It will go where the Spirit wants
it to go.

Make prayer a part of every Couple Talk Time. Follow my guidelines, and you'll be amazed at the intimacy God will give you.

Next, let's take a look at another gold mine of spiritual intimacy:
spiritual conversations.

ASK YOURSELVES THESE QUESTIONS

1. How busy are your lives? Are you pulling apart as a couple?

2. How often do you pray together? When do you pray together?
   When you pray, what do you pray about?

3. What are your fears and concerns about praying in your Couple
   Talk Times? How hard will this be for you to do? Why?

4. Of all the guidelines about praying together I shared, which one
   sounds best for you? Why? Which one would be the most difficult for you? Why?

CHAPTER 20

SPIRITUAL CONVERSATIONS
AS A COUPLE

ONE OF THE MOST DIFFICULT THINGS for a Clam is to share his spiritual life, his relationship with Jesus, with his wife. Not just difficult. Really, really difficult. In my experience, a Clam has four major reasons why he does not open up and talk with his wife about his spirituality. The following dialogue reveals these reasons and my responses.

Clam: My dad never shared his spiritual life with my mom. Or with any of us kids.

Me: That was some powerful modeling. What was your parents' marriage like?

Clam: They stayed together, but they weren't close.

Me: No surprise there. If you don't share spiritually as a couple, you can't be close on a deep level.

Clam: It's not my personality to share personal things. I automatically keep what I think and feel inside. And my spiritual life is very personal.

Me: What have I told you that your wife needs from you more than anything else?

Clam: To know me. The real me. Who I am inside.

Me: Right. If you don't open up to her, she won't feel loved by you. And your relationship with Jesus is the most important part of you.

Clam: My spiritual life is very private. It's just between me and Jesus.

Me: Genesis 2:24 describes marriage as the one-flesh relationship. That means complete unity. No secrets. She has the right to know about your relationship with Jesus. No one else does, but she does.

Clam: It will be hard to admit my spiritual struggles and weaknesses to my wife. I'll feel weak and less of a man.

Me: No, you won't. You'll feel like a real man. She'll love and respect you for being that honest and vulnerable. And she'll support you and encourage you in your spiritual life.

The Clam, the Crowbar, and God

I spent the first three-quarters of this book teaching you how to develop emotional intimacy. If you follow my strategies, I firmly believe your conversations will be deeper and more personal.

Now that you can create closeness in your conversations, it's time to learn how to talk on an even deeper level. The spiritual level.

When you talk about your spiritual life, your relationship with God, you tap a gold mine of intimacy. When I tell Sandy how God is working in my life, I open a door so she can see inside me. When I share with her how I'm doing in my relationship with Jesus, she really knows me at the core of my being. Because Jesus is the center of my life, I'm sharing the most important and personal part of me.

This will not come as a shock, but communicating with your spouse about spiritual matters does not come naturally. Nothing in marriage comes naturally. You need to learn how to build spiritual conversations.

Just as with prayer, I want you to include spiritual conversations in every Couple Talk Time. Even a few minutes of spiritual talk will go a long way in the department of intimacy.

Your conversations about spiritual matters will take place on at least three different levels. Let's look at them.

Level One: The Personal Level

You learn to tell your partner, regularly and in detail, about your spiritual life: what you're doing in your daily quiet time with God, insights you've gained in your Bible reading, and how you're applying the Bible to your life. You need to talk about your spiritual victories—those times when God gave you the power and courage to share Christ with a coworker, overcome a weakness, or help a friend in need.

You also need to admit your spiritual defeats—those times when you failed to obey God, or read the Bible regularly for a day or more, or impact those around you for Christ. When Satan attacks you, and he will, tell your partner and pray about it together.

Each of you can share how God is working in your individual lives and how He is using daily events to guide and teach you. People frequently say to me, "Dave, I just live my life. Things happen. I know God is in charge, but He's not really all that involved in the details of my life, is He?" I reply, "Oh, yes, He is—if you know Him."

Once you have a relationship with God, God is with you twenty-four hours a day. "For he has said, 'I will never leave you nor forsake you'" (Hebrews 13:5). He's guiding and leading you. He's creating events every day to teach you, to develop your character, and to build your faith in Him. God is choreographing your entire life! When you open your eyes and see what He is doing, your whole perspective changes. No day is ever again routine because your sovereign God is the director of every scene, every event, every interaction.

This is not only good for your personal spiritual life, but it also provides an inexhaustible supply of conversational material for you and your spouse. You can come home every day and say, "Guess what God did in my life today!"

In fact, He made lots of things happen in your day. All for you! When you start noticing God's involvement in your day, you'll have things to talk about. You'll have some terrific conversations that are personal, revealing, stimulating, and encouraging.

Level Two: The Relationship Level

You can also talk about how God is working in your marriage or your dating relationship. He is intimately involved in the details of your relationship. About once or twice a month, ask each other some searching spiritual questions: "What is God teaching us as a couple?" "What does God want us to learn from each other?" "How is He guiding us through painful times in our relationship?" "For what good, positive things can we thank Him?" "Are we pleasing Him in our relationship?"

What you're doing is evaluating your relationship from a spiritual perspective. If you are believers, you believe that at its core, your marriage is a spiritual relationship, and God uses events in it to build your faith—to mold your marriage into a dynamic, one-flesh relationship that shows the world that God is alive and well.

Do you know there are couples who go days, weeks, months, or even years without ever talking about how God is working in their lives and marriages? Of course you do. Perhaps you've never done this kind of sharing yourselves. Most couples don't, because they don't know how spiritual conversations will benefit their marriage.

Level Three: The External Level

At this level, you share concerns about other people: family, pastors, friends, coworkers, neighbors, missionaries, people in the news, and political leaders. You dialogue about the physical health, relationship problems, and spiritual health of persons you care about.

You talk about what you can learn from the lives of others—their mistakes, their hardships, or their steps of faith. There are valuable lessons to be learned from watching and talking about the lives of Christians and non-Christians around you.

Getting a Clam to Talk about the Spiritual

Let's be honest. It's easy to explain these three levels, but it's tough to actually do them. I can hear you women readers: "He won't talk to me about his trip to the home improvement store! How can I get him to talk about spiritual things?" I have some strategies that will help.

Because of our Clam-Crowbar differences, regular conversations between partners can be difficult. Men and women approach spiritual topics quite differently too. Conversations about the spiritual are even more difficult because they require more openness and vulnerability. I must say most husbands aren't known for these traits. Logic is the way most men initially respond to God and spiritual events. They rationalize. They focus on the facts. They plan a course of action. They *think* first. Conversely, most women initially respond with emotion. They go with their instincts, their gut reactions, their intuition. They *feel* first.

Men need time and space to process spiritual matters. They respond more slowly to questions of faith. Women respond to God and His truth more quickly. Women use emotions to process spiritual truth. While the man uses a paper and pencil to figure out how God wants him to respond, the woman hits a few computer keys and prints out a response in a flash.

Men are less verbal about faith than women. This shouldn't come as a shock to you women, since men are less verbal than you about almost everything. It's tough—extremely tough—for a man to talk on a spiritual level with his wife. But he can learn how, and you can help him by following some basic communication principles.

You'll recognize most of these principles from earlier chapters.

Start with Prayer

I began this spiritual bonding section with prayer because it's a great way to prepare for a spiritual dialogue. Even if you pray out loud and he doesn't, the act of talking to God is an effective warm-up for a spiritual conversation. Prayer puts the man in a spiritual mood and makes him aware of God's presence.

Ask Him to Listen

Before you begin to talk, ask the man to listen to you and respond to what you say. Tell him you really need his attention and his reaction. Tell him that by being a good sounding board, he'll help you grow spiritually. Most men don't naturally like to talk, but they do like to feel needed. If he does a decent job of listening and provides a few responses, he'll connect with you in the spiritual area and be drawn into the conversation.

Be Brief

Another thing, ladies: Be brief. Speak for two or three minutes, and then be quiet. Do not talk on and on, hoping that your volume of words will increase the chances of getting a response. All it will do is increase the chances of his brain shutting down. Especially in a conversation about the spiritual, less is more. Make a few comments, and then give him a chance to respond.

Keep Mr. Logic on Track

If he responds with logic, which he's likely to do, interrupt him by saying, "Honey, that's logic. I need listening and understanding. Okay?" If you don't cut in and get him back on track, the conversation won't go anywhere. And you'll feel hurt, resentful, and completely not understood.

He's not being malicious with his logic. In fact, he thinks he's doing a public service when he says something like: "Sweetheart, you're just too upset about this. God is a loving God, and it doesn't help to doubt Him. Just let it go, and everything will work out just fine." Statements like these are not a public service; they are a public nuisance. Thank him for trying to help, but tell him that you want him to get back in the listening mode.

Ask Him Questions

After you've spoken to him about spiritual matters for a few minutes, it's okay to ask him a few questions and bring up a few issues about which you'd like him to comment. It's the way you ask him to respond that's important. Use words like these: "Honey, you don't have to respond right now." (He wasn't going to anyway, but this relieves any pressure he might be feeling.) "When you're ready, I'd like to hear what your reaction is to what I said."

It's essential to use the words "when you're ready" with a man, because he needs to feel in control. He must respond in his time and on his terms. You've given him that manly right, and he'll appreciate it. It doesn't guarantee a response, but it increases the odds of getting one.

Let Him Ride the Spiritual Train

You already know that a man needs time to process what you say to him and figure out how to react. He has to think about and organize any kind of a deeper, more meaningful response. He must ride the train to sort out his own internal thoughts and feelings.

Because the spiritual area is so personal and important, his train trips will take longer than for regular topics of conversation. Give him the time he needs. He'll come back to you when he's ready and has something to say.

You Talk Spiritually in Stages

Just as in your own nonspiritual, everyday conversations, the two of you will only begin to talk on a deeper spiritual level in stages. Deep, intimate conversation—spiritual or otherwise—does not happen in one sitting.

The best spiritual conversations occur over the course of a week as you keep revisiting the same topics. The woman brings up a spiritual issue, and the man listens and reflects. He rides the train to process and pray to God to help him with his reaction, then returns and restarts the conversation with his response. The woman reacts to what he says, and then he rides the train again.

Sound familiar? It will take three or four talks on the same spiritual topic before the man *and* the woman get deep and fully explore their spiritual reactions and insights.

Use the Pad to Generate Spiritual Topics

All you Clams, I've already explained how writing thoughts and ideas on the pad or typing them into your smartphone can help you begin conversations with your Crowbar. Now I want you to do the same thing with spiritual topics.

You have spiritual insights, ideas, and feelings about God, your relationship to Him, Bible truths you read, and questions that come up during the day. You see God working in your life. The problem is, just as with other daily issues, by the end of the day you can't remember your experiences in these areas.

So, Clams, don't trust your memory. Throughout the day, as you notice the hand of God in your life, record these experiences on your pad or in your electronic device. This way they are not lost forever.

That night, or at your next Couple Talk Time, you'll have a list of spiritual things you have thought about that you can share. Your woman will be thrilled. God will be pleased. The two of you will connect spiritually.

Dave Clarke's Pad

As I write these words, my day is almost over. Here's a list of God-inspired events that I recorded:

1. In my individual quiet time this morning, I read about suffering for Christ in 1 Peter. I haven't suffered for Christ very many times in my life. I wonder if sharing Christ with three of my neighbors who did not welcome my words about Christ would qualify as suffering?

2. I prayed about the ongoing negotiations for the purchase of a new home. This process isn't suffering for Christ, but it is definitely suffering! Despite my feelings of anger and incredible frustration, I am trying to give it to God.

3. I had a great phone conversation with a fellow Christian counselor in Moultrie, Georgia, named David Brown. He's a godly man with a heart for helping couples. We talked about my upcoming marriage seminar he is sponsoring and what we'd like to see God do that weekend.

When Sandy and I sit down tonight to talk, I will share these items. It'll be interesting to see where these spiritual topics take us in conversation. We'll have a stimulating talk, and we'll bond spiritually.

As you pray and have spiritual conversations with your partner, your spiritual bond will continue to grow stronger.

Since God wants you to be as spiritually close as possible, there is one more area of spiritual intimacy I need to cover.

ASK YOURSELVES THESE QUESTIONS

1. How many spiritual conversations—on the personal level, the relationship level, and the external level—have you two had in the past six months?

2. If you seldom, if ever, talk about spiritual subjects, why do you think you don't? Has anyone in your life—family, friends, pastors, authors you have read—ever talked about developing spiritual conversations as a couple?

3. Can you relate to the typical initial responses men (logic first) and women (emotion first) have to talking about spiritual issues? Discuss how each of you usually responds to spiritual subjects.

4. Mrs. Crowbar, how difficult will it be to follow my tips to help your Clam open up in a conversation about spiritual areas? Which tip or strategy will be the hardest for you to follow?

5. Mr. Clam, are you willing to (1) record your spiritual experiences and thoughts during the day and (2) then share them with your wife? What will get in the way of doing these two actions?

6. Choose one spiritual topic right now and agree to talk about it in your four Couple Talk Times this week.

CHAPTER 21

READING THE BIBLE
AS A COUPLE

I WAS SITTING WITH A MAN AND his wife in my office. It was near the end of the therapy session, and we were discussing the spiritual aspect of their relationship. They admitted they were both spiritually flat.

"We don't feel close to God," the husband said. "We can't figure out His will for our lives and relationship. We're just not experiencing His power in our marriage."

"How often do you read the Bible?" I asked them.

The man thought for a moment, then said, "To be honest, I read the Bible about twice a week."

"And I usually read it five times a week," the wife responded.

"No, you don't understand. I mean, how often do you read the Bible *together*?"

They looked at each other and back at me. Finally the wife replied, "Well, actually, we don't read the Bible together."

I shared with them my conviction that reading the Bible together is a primary means of accessing God's power. I tried to persuade them that reading the Word of God together would invigorate the spiritual part of their relationship. It would bring them closer to God. It would make clear His will for their marriage. It would give them a collective energy boost.

I didn't give this husband and wife a hard time for not reading the Bible together. In fact, I told them I could relate to their situation. I admitted that my wife and I didn't read the Bible together for years. We didn't realize what we were missing. We didn't know that we were choosing to leave a huge power source untapped. It was like trying to operate our home without any electricity. We were running our marriage manually, using our own energy. And it didn't work too well.

I told this couple about the Bible reading program that Sandy and I have developed, and they decided to try it. Over the course of two months, they sat down and read God's Word together. They discussed the passages they read, and they helped each other apply them. Simply put, they allowed the Bible's power to transform their marriage.

At the end of the two months, they were much closer to God and to each other. They had found the power to communicate, to resolve conflict, and to love each other much more deeply.

The Bible Brings Down Your Walls

When you read and study and talk about the Bible together, the walls between you come down. God's Word cuts through every defense, every barrier, and every Clam-Crowbar difference. The Bible will bring you closer than you've ever been.

Most people don't think of the Bible as a direct avenue to male-female intimacy, but that is exactly what it is. Or at least it can be, if the two of you regularly read and study it. Hebrews 4:12 says, "For the word of God is living and active, sharper than any two-edged sword, piercing to the division of soul and spirit, of joints and of marrow, and discerning the thoughts and intentions of the heart."

Wow! The picture here is of the sharpest blade in the universe cutting deep and exposing everything about a person. God's Word will reveal who you really are inside. When two hearts and minds are revealed, intimacy is the result.

When you read and study the Bible on your own, what happens? God speaks to you. God reveals deep, meaningful things about you. God tells you what He wants you to do in your life and in your relationships.

When you read the Bible *together*, your partner learns all these intimate and personal things about you, too!

Get a Good Study Bible

To get started, all you need is one basic tool. You each need a good study Bible. Select one with helpful notes that give the historical context, explain the meaning of key verses, and list other verses on the same topic. I recommend the New American Standard Bible (NASB) or the New King James Version (NKJV).

Ask your pastor what version he recommends. And you both need to use the same exact version. Don't confuse yourselves with different wordings. An opposite-sex relationship is confusing enough.

Read One Passage at a Time

To make your time together in reading the Bible profitable, you should read slowly and carefully. Read and study one short passage (one verse or several verses) at a time. Study Bibles usually divide the text into paragraphs for easy reading. Concentrate on the passage, linger on it, and try to discern what God is teaching you through His Word.

Speed is not important. Understanding and application are important. It defeats the purpose to race through Scripture at breakneck speed. Always keep in mind that these are actually God-inspired words, His Word to us.

Some couples have told me proudly, "We're reading through the

Bible in one year!" My response has been, "That's great. What are you learning?" They reply, "We don't know, but we're moving right along! We'll be done by December thirty-first."

Take your time as you read, like time with a good friend or trusted mentor. Zero in on one passage, and let it sink in. Let it get to your brain and then continue to your heart and your will.

Choose Passages from a Variety of Sources

There are a variety of ways to choose Bible passages to read, meditate on, and study. Your individual quiet times with God can call your attention to verses that you might want to look at further with your partner. As you read your Bible alone, the Holy Spirit might use a certain verse to convict you of something you need to correct or eliminate in your life. Jot down that verse and share it with your spouse at your next reading session.

Your pastor's sermons are a gold mine of verses for your Bible study. Take advantage of the hours he has spent researching and studying. If a verse he uses impacts you, talk to your partner about it during the week.

Small group Bible studies are another rich source of discussion material. Beth Moore has a series of excellent Bible studies. Bible Study Fellowship has wonderful studies for men and women. Or you may be in a Bible study at your church.

Radio and television teachers can also provide verses for your joint study. I love Chuck Swindoll, David Jeremiah, and Tony Evans. These men can flat-out preach, and they handle the Bible superbly. You can listen to a radio preacher during the day and come back home that evening with a verse or two for you and your mate to study.

Decide Which Bible Books to Read

It's okay to read and study passages from different books of the Bible. One week you may be in Matthew, the next week in 1 Corinthians, then in Daniel, and so on. But I recommend that you spend at least half of your study time reading a particular book of the Bible from beginning to end. You must take small chunks, a few verses at a time. This approach provides continuity and a smoother flow of Scripture. You'll get a good, solid picture of the book's overall message and purpose, and you won't have to worry about which passage you'll read next, because you'll just pick up where you left off.

If you're new to Bible reading and studying as a couple, there are certain books of the Bible I suggest you start with. With its beautiful language and short, wisdom-filled verses about life and relationships, Proverbs is a great book for couples. Paul's epistles—including Galatians, Ephesians, Philippians, and Colossians—are concise, easy to read, and intensely practical. You may consider them as letters to you as believers. I especially urge you to read the Gospels—Matthew, Mark, Luke, and John. Reading these accounts of Jesus' life and ministry is like sitting at the Master's feet as He teaches and enlightens.

How to Read and Study the Bible Together

Sandy and I have developed a simple, straightforward system for reading and studying the Bible. It doesn't take much time, and it takes into account the Clam-Crowbar differences.

It works for us, and I think it will work for you. Working as a team, you follow four steps over a two-week period.

Step One: Read

First, you sit down early in the week—on a Sunday or Monday evening—and one partner reads aloud the passage of Scripture you have selected. You then take a minute or two to silently meditate on the passage. Ask God to speak to you through His Word.

Then each of you briefly discusses your response to the passage. What does the passage mean? What is God saying to you? What thoughts and emotions does the passage trigger?

It's common for the woman to have an immediate reaction and for the man to not have much to say. I know that comes as a shock, ladies. He'll say, "I don't know" or "I'm not sure."

It's perfectly normal for the man to not be able to give a response at this first meeting. He hasn't processed yet. He's got until Friday!

Ladies, don't press him for a response right away:

"What's your reaction to the passage, Bob?"

"It's the Word of God, Bob!"

"God and I are waiting, Bob!"

Ladies (Crowbars), back off. Let him ride the train and find out what the verse means to him. The truth is, you both need time to get the deeper meaning of the passage.

At the end of this Read meeting, you do three things. First, you schedule the next meeting, the Discuss meeting, for Friday or Saturday evening. Second, you pray, while holding hands, that God will speak to each of you through the passage over the next five or six days.

Third, you record the passage on a three-by-five card or in your phone.

Step Two: Meditate

During the next five or six days, you each carry the passage with you wherever you go. Read the verse and meditate on it at least once a day. This could be part of your daily personal quiet time. Ask God to show you what the verse means to you and how He wants you to apply it. Record—on your card or in your phone—what you believe God is saying to you from the verses.

Step Three: Discuss

At the end of the week, meet again to share the results of the meditation and reflection. At this meeting, you'll both have some things, some deeper things, to say. The woman will have more to say because she always has more to say. The man will have more to say because he's had time to process.

The reality is, your week of meditation on the verses will get both of you to a deeper level.

Read—from your card or your phone—what you recorded during the week. *Here is what God is saying to me through this passage. Here's what it means for my life, our relationship, or our family.*

Tell each other what you will do to apply the passage in the coming week. Agree to record how you specifically applied what you learned and what happened when you did. Pray briefly that God will help you both follow through in your application of His Word.

Step Four: Apply

The final step is to meet approximately one week later to share how God used the passage in your daily experiences. Each of you read your comments about how you applied God's Word. Describe what you learned. You may have to admit that you did not apply what you learned, and talk about what hindered you from doing so. If either partner wasn't able to fully apply the passage, extend the process another week.

Even when you have practiced this four-step process and gained some proficiency at it, you will not implement it in every two-week period of the year. That is too much to expect. But reading and applying a passage once a month, or even once every two months, will be a tremendous accomplishment and will greatly bless your relationship.

The Bible, the Blonde, and Me

To briefly illustrate this four-step process, I'll give you a window into one occasion when Sandy and I followed this plan.

A few years ago, we were going through a very painful, traumatic time. You know how bad things tend to hit all at once? We were dealing with three major life events at the same time.

To protect those involved, I'll give you the overall sketch and not the details. We left our church after seventeen years. That would have been tough enough, but we also had to face two family crises. It was awful and, at times, overwhelming.

God led me to a passage that helped Sandy and me get through months of pain and heartache: "Count it all joy, my brothers, when you meet trials of various kinds, for you know that the testing of your faith produces steadfastness. And let steadfastness have its full effect, that you may be perfect and complete, lacking in nothing" (James 1:2-4).

We were facing a serious trial, and we knew our faith was being tested. But not for no reason. If we could persevere, we would be closer to being mature and complete in our faith in God.

I'll share what I recorded during my week of meditation (Step Two):

- My career was not as important as my family.

- This pain would give me more empathy for my clients.

- This trial would bring Sandy and me closer; we'd go through it together.

- I needed to spend time with one of my daughters.

- This traumatic time would bring me closer to God.

With Sandy's help, I decided to apply James 1:2-4 the next week in a very specific way. I stopped seeing clients after 5 p.m. This allowed me to focus on our daughter individually several days each week, and also have time with Sandy and the other kids.

God honored this scheduling decision and blessed my clinical practice even more.

This is just one application of this passage. Sandy and I both applied it in a number of ways over the course of that year.

This concludes my crash course in spiritual bonding. In the next chapter, I will address a very common and painful scenario: "But my partner can't or won't spiritually bond."

ASK YOURSELVES THESE QUESTIONS

1. Do you read and study the Bible on your own on a regular basis? If so, how is it benefiting you?

2. How often do you read and study the Bible together? What stops you from doing this?

3. Which of my four steps for reading and studying the Bible (Read, Meditate, Discuss, Apply) would be the most difficult for you? Why?

4. Choose a passage right now and commit to following my four-step process over the next two weeks.

CHAPTER 22

"BUT MY PARTNER CAN'T OR WON'T SPIRITUALLY BOND"

When your partner shows no interest in building a spiritual bond with you, it hurts. It hurts deeply. Here's a dialogue I had with a wife who wanted desperately to bond spiritually with her husband.

Wife: My husband continues to reject all my efforts to create a spiritual bond between us. I've tried everything I can think of: prayed my heart out, begged and pleaded, gotten angry, cried in front of him, dragged him to seminars, asked him to read books, met with our pastor. Nothing has worked. I feel hopeless. I know what we're missing, but he has no clue.

Me: The direct approach doesn't work. The more you try, the more he resists. I have a different strategy that I've seen work many times. If you follow it, before God you will know you did your absolute best to generate a spiritual bond with him.

It's very common to be in a spiritually challenged romantic relationship. What I mean by that is this: You are a committed, growing Christian, but your partner—whether you are married or not—is either not a Christian or not interested in a spiritual bond with you.

The Bad News

The bad news is that one of the main obstacles to spiritual bonding is a partner who's not interested. Perhaps the person is not a Christian, and therefore spiritual bonding between you is not possible. Or maybe the person is a Christian but just doesn't want to develop the spiritual part of your relationship. Either way, you're stuck and unable to experience the deepest intimacy possible in your relationship.

The Good News

The good news is that there are a number of practical, effective things you can do to motivate your partner in the area of spiritual intimacy. Over the years, I've developed a list of the top ten ways to draw a partner into spiritual bonding. Whatever your situation—trying to lead your partner to Christ or trying to get your Christian partner to spiritually bond with you—these same steps apply. If you follow them, you'll be doing the best you can to influence your loved one.

If You're Not Married

If you're dating someone who is not a Christian, I have a very tough recommendation for you: Break up, and break up now.

Continuing in the relationship will only deepen your love and commitment and make it harder to break up. There is no guarantee your partner will ever become a Christian.

Or if your Christian partner won't spiritually bond with you, break up.

I don't give this advice to break up easily and with no concern for your feelings. You love this person, so walking away will hurt deeply. You are letting go of your hopes and dreams for the relationship.

But breaking up will spare you and your partner from the deeper pain of a marriage with no spiritual bond. And the breakup may motivate your partner to seriously consider beginning a relationship with Jesus.

You don't have to stay with this person, and I strongly believe you should not.

Move on, and with God's blessing and guidance, find a person who is a growing believer and will spiritually bond with you.

Sometimes my clients feel stuck because they have children with their partner. That's certainly a more complicated situation with no perfect solution, and it's vitally important to think through the needs of the children. But I often tell my clients that they don't have to stay in a relationship with this person. To make sure they handle the situation the right way and protect themselves, their partner, and the children, I tell them it's best to seek Christian counseling before doing anything else.

If You're Married

Marriage is a sacred relationship, so my advice to those of you who are married is different. The ten principles are the same, but how long you do them is different. Whether your spouse is a Christian or not, God wants you to stay married.

I recommend you continue to apply my ten principles for as long as it takes. For as long as you both shall live. You don't have a six-month campaign. You have a lifelong campaign.

How This Chapter Is Written

I'm writing as if you are married, though you may not be. My principles apply equally to married and unmarried couples.

Also, I'm writing this chapter to a woman who is trying to motivate a man. Frankly, statistics show that it is a woman who is more likely to be reading this book. And far more women than men feel the need to spiritually bond. Obviously, there are plenty of men who need help attracting their women to the spiritual bonding process, and all of my principles can be used with women, too.

The "Don'ts"

Do not pressure him in any way. As you already know, Clams do not respond to pressure. Don't plead. Don't beg. Don't cry. Don't yell. Don't get angry. Don't lecture. Don't keep asking him to attend church or other spiritual activities or events.

Your best chance to influence him spiritually is a low-key, no-direct-pressure approach.

Don't feel bad if you have resorted to using all of these pressure tactics. Almost everyone does. The stakes—eternity in heaven and the best possible marriage here on earth—couldn't be higher. So it's easy to press too hard. Just stop the pressure now, and try my way.

These ten action steps are a campaign that I've seen work many times.

Step One: Present Your Case

When you first bring up the issue of spiritual bonding with your husband, your approach must be logical and practical. Most men do not respond to emotion. You may express your emotions, but it's best to do so in a low-key, nonthreatening way.

You must also avoid any hint that you feel you are spiritually superior or a more knowledgeable Christian. If he feels the least bit inferior or thinks that you see him this way, his defenses will go up, and your chances of success will go down.

Before you even broach the subject, you must understand that he will not respond right away. You know that, don't you? He won't say, "Honey, great idea! I wish I'd thought of this spiritual bonding stuff myself. Let's do it. Take my hand, and let's pray right now." There are perhaps five men in the entire world who would respond this way. And you're not married to one of them. Men, by nature, have a delayed reaction to serious, deep subjects (except, maybe, why their football team is losing).

Tell your husband that you want to discuss something important with him. Make him wait a day or two, so he knows it's something big. Then sit down together, and ask him to listen and hear you out. Tell him you don't want him to respond now (not that he would anyway). This makes him feel in control and gives him time to process what you say.

Present your case for spiritual bonding in a simple, straightforward, and brief way. Do not go over fifteen minutes. Cover the benefits: "It will help us grow spiritually as individuals. It will create physical and emotional intimacy in our marriage. It will lead to God's blessing." Tell him that your marriage is not what it could be. It is missing something. Tell him you've read a wonderful book by a top Christian psychologist, and you've realized that *spiritual bonding* is what's missing.

What you're doing is creating in him a desire, a need, for spiritual intimacy. You're not inventing his need for this. It's there. You're just trying to get the man to see it.

If you're struggling with a specific problem in your marriage, bring it up in this initial conversation. Tell your husband that putting God at the center of your relationship is the key to solving the problem. With God, you can solve anything.

Finish your opening statement by asking him to think and pray about what you've said. Ask him to give you a response when he's ready. There's a high likelihood that he will not get back to you. Or, if he does, that he won't be willing yet to engage in a spiritual bonding process. What you've done is clearly state the need, establish spiritual bonding as a priority, and set the stage for my nine other strategies.

Step Two: Be a Dynamic Christian

Model a Spirit-filled, vibrant Christian life. (Obviously, this should be genuine and not just a ploy.) Let your husband witness your joy in Christ. Your spouse won't be interested in Christ or the Christian walk if your spiritual life is blah. If it doesn't work for you, what makes you think he will want it? You are the best advertisement for a relationship with Jesus that your husband will ever see.

The Bible teaches that it is possible to win a spouse to Christ without even saying a word. You can't make a person want to be spiritual, but you can draw your unbelieving or spiritually apathetic spouse to Christ by exhibiting a spirituality that is alive and authentic (see 1 Corinthians 7:12-16 and 1 Peter 3:1-7).

Let him see you meeting regularly with God for personal prayer, Bible study, and devotions. If you have children, lead family devotions at least once a week. Invite him, but hold the family devotions even if he refuses to attend or is opposed to them. Every night, pray with each child before bedtime.

Attend church with the kids, even if your spouse will not go with you. Go even if he discourages you from going or tells you flatly not to go. Some well-meaning Christian wives allow their non-Christian husbands to prevent them from attending church. They say that in doing this, they are obeying the Bible's instruction to be submissive to their husbands and live in harmony with others. I say, baloney. You have a higher law to obey. God wants every Christian to be part of a local church body (see Hebrews 10:25).

You need to worship God with others. Your children need to learn how to walk with Jesus. You need spiritual teaching and interaction with and encouragement and support from others who love the Lord. It's also a good idea to join a women's Bible study. Your church may have one, or you could join an excellent parachurch ministry such as Bible Study Fellowship. It is hard—incredibly hard—to live with a man who's not leading you spiritually. You need the support that a church and Bible study group can give you.

Step Three: Spiritually Bond with a Friend

Find a good friend of your gender, a fellow Christian, with whom you can spiritually bond. The two of you can follow many of the steps outlined in the preceding chapters. Praying together, reading God's Word, being accountable to one another, and having spiritual conversations will be a source of tremendous encouragement and support.

And don't forget venting. From time to time, you'll need to ask this person to listen as you "dump" the accumulated emotions that come with living with a spiritually dead or spiritually uninterested spouse. As a practical matter, there will be times when this spiritual friendship will be the only thing that keeps you going.

This venting does not include heavy criticism of your husband or saying a bunch of negative things about him. It is periodically sharing the honest pain you feel because of the lack of spiritual bonding in your marriage.

The person you vent with is someone you can trust, someone who won't think badly of your husband, and someone who will always support your marriage. This kind of venting with this kind of person will help clean out your resentments and keep you committed to your marriage.

Bonding with a close friend will enrich your own personal spiritual life. You cannot experience significant spiritual growth alone. No one can. We all have a need to spiritually bond with someone. If it can't be your spouse right now, for the time being it will have to be with a same-sex friend.

Step Four: Share Your Spiritual Life with Him

Ask your husband if it's okay for you to share your spiritual life with him periodically. Assure him that it will take only five minutes once or twice a week and all he has to do is listen. Tell him you're not looking for a response (of course, you'd love a positive one, but you're not going to ask him for one). Tell him that your spiritual life is an integral part of you and that you'll feel closer to him if you can share it. Tell him that you need this. Men like to be needed. It's a rare man who will refuse this reasonable request.

Share how God is guiding you and teaching you. Reveal spiritual triumphs and disappointments. Mention what you are praying about, and tell him God's answers to your prayers. Don't let his apparent lack of interest discourage you. Ignore it entirely, and continue as though he were interested. Keep on letting him see—in small glimpses—what God is doing in your life. Speak only about yourself, your feelings and experiences. Don't ask him questions, and don't try to elicit a response from him.

Your brief spiritual updates will expose him to God and what He is doing in your life. He'll become more aware of God's presence. It may draw him closer to you and to God. Also, you are modeling how to live for Christ and how to talk spiritually. He might just catch on and want to get more involved with you.

Step Five: Tell Him What He Is Missing

The average husband is satisfied with far less intimacy in his marriage than his wife is. Your husband is probably like this. He thinks everything's fine—just peachy keen—while you're dying inside. He doesn't realize how important spiritual bonding is. He just doesn't get it. To help him get it, you have to upset his comfortable "We're doing okay" attitude about the marriage. He needs to know what you are missing, and what he is missing.

Tell him when you see God working in his life: "Jim, I think God's talking to you through this situation at work." Point out how Christ can help him in difficult times: "You don't have to face this alone. God promises to always be with us." Use examples from the lives of friends and neighbors to illustrate spiritual truths: "God really saved the Smiths' marriage. Sally told me that their faith pulled them through that hard time." Let him know how much better your marriage could be with spiritual bonding: "I think we'd have a much closer relationship if we prayed together."

Be sure not to say these things in a mean or sarcastic way. Be honest and gentle and humble. Your attitude should be one of longing on his behalf, but especially of sadness and disappointment for him. You know that his life and your marriage could be so much better with spiritual intimacy, if you shared your faith in Christ and your walk with Him with one another. So you continue to be the best wife you can be. But you don't pretend that you are completely satisfied and fulfilled.

Also, don't make these comments frequently. You don't want to be a pest. Pick the occasions as God guides. Just say a sentence or two, and then drop it and move on.

Step Six: Express Your Feelings and Desires

It is essential to tell your husband periodically how you feel about the fact that you are not sharing Christ as a couple or that you are not enjoying spiritual intimacy. Because of this, you feel a sense of longing, loss, and grief.

If you stuff these emotions, they will turn into frustration, bitterness, and resentment. You will pull back emotionally, and possibly physically, from your partner. You will react in anger to small mistakes your partner makes. The growing discontent and resentment inside will begin breaking you down physically, emotionally, and spiritually. As time goes on, you will entertain thoughts of leaving the marriage.

To prevent these reactions and remain committed to your marriage partner, you must clean your system from time to time by expressing your emotions. As Scripture teaches, speak the truth in love (see Ephesians 4:15) directly to your partner. Don't make a scene. Don't lose control, yell, or put pressure on your spouse.

When you feel painful emotions building up inside you, write a letter to your husband that honestly and gently releases your pain. Here is a letter written by a wife to her non-Christian husband:

Dear Bob,

As you know, from time to time I need to write you this kind of letter. It helps me release my emotions and stay close to you. My faith in God is such an important part of my life. I know you don't understand it, but I really could not live without God. I feel hurt, angry, and sad because we cannot share a bond in Christ. I'm sorry for the way I acted last week. I get too intense sometimes and think I can force you to believe in Jesus and who He is and what He did for you.

I love you for who you are, and I'm thankful for the good things in our relationship. I just can't help my desire for us to add the spiritual part to our marriage so we can truly be one, completely.

Well, I'm done. Please don't feel pressured by it. If and when you trust Christ, it will have to be your decision.

Thanks for having patience with me. I love you.

Cindy

If your husband has trusted Christ, you'll follow the same approach, but your letters will focus on your intense longing for him to join you in adding this spiritual dimension to your marriage. You may express your feelings verbally if you want. However, a letter is easier, less threatening to the man, and still gets the job done.

Whether you talk or write, this is one-way communication. As you can see in my sample letter, you make it clear that he doesn't have to respond. In addition to washing away your painful emotions, this one-way technique keeps the issue of spiritual bonding before him. He must face again and again your need in this area.

Step Seven: Ask for Small Steps

Don't make the mistake of asking him to do too much, too soon. Spiritual bonding is hard for a man. He may not take a major role in the bonding for some time. He certainly will not lead right away. It's easy to overwhelm your husband and make him feel inadequate. Don't do that.

Here's what you do: Ask him for small steps—baby steps—as you begin the process. Tell him that *you* would like to pray, and look to him for an indication that that's fine with him. If he's okay with it, pray for a minute or two. On a date or just before the church service begins, ask him to pray briefly with you. Ask him to pray for thirty seconds with you about whatever he'd like to bring up. If he asks what he can pray for, smile and say, "Why don't you thank God for your beautiful wife, whom you love so very much?"

When the man makes the smallest move toward spiritual intimacy, praise him for it. Your immediate and heartfelt appreciation will reinforce the behavior and build his confidence. It's not quite like training a seal, but it's close. Give him affection, notes, or a special dinner. After he's carried out a small spiritual bonding behavior, tell him, "I feel closer to you" or "When you join me in our prayer time, my respect for you just climbs." These are true statements, and he needs to hear them. It is also a great reinforcement for you to mention in the presence of others something he has done when you have been doing some spiritual bonding exercises. Knowing he is pleasing you will please him.

Assure him that you're pleased with progress and any step in the direction of spiritual bonding. Tell him you're not expecting him to be Billy Graham or some other renowned Christian. Let him know that you certainly don't have all the answers—that you want to work together on achieving spiritual intimacy.

Step Eight: Surround Him with Christians
Build relationships with other Christians, and do your best to expose your husband to these godly people. Invite Christian couples to your home, especially those who have children the same ages as your children. Find men who are walking with Jesus and doing at least some spiritual bonding with their wives. Ask these men to invite your husband to play

golf or a sport your husband enjoys, attend a sporting event, come to men's ministry meetings at the church, or go to a Christian event.

Your children can also be great examples to their dad. As you nurture the spiritual lives of your kids, your husband is bound to notice the good, positive changes in their lives. Their lives will speak volumes about Jesus and what He does in a life given to Him. Involve the children in church programs—Sunday Bible classes for their age groups, Awana, and youth group. Have the kids ask Dad to help them with their spiritual lessons and projects. One woman Sandy and I know had her kids recite their memory verses to her non-Christian husband. It is impossible not to be affected by your children quoting God's Word. God promises that His Word will not return to Him without accomplishing what He desires (see Isaiah 55:11).

Step Nine: Use Times of Crisis and Pain

When times of crisis strike your marriage and family, and they will, seize those moments to help your husband see his need for Christ and for spiritual bonding. He will be the most open to change when life is at its most painful. In these tough times, ask him to join you in prayer. If he refuses, go ahead and—in front of him—cry out to God for guidance, healing, strength, and comfort. As your spouse sees you broken and reaching out to God, he may begin to comfort you. And in doing so, he may for the first time feel a spiritual bond with you and the Lord.

Step Ten: Pray

Pray regularly for your spouse, or if you are in a serious relationship that may be headed toward marriage, pray for your partner. Pray on your own. Pray with your same-sex spiritual bonding partner. Pray at Bible studies with your fellow believers. Pray at church with two or three others as indicated in Matthew 18:19-20. Ask others you know and trust to pray for your spouse. Never underestimate the power of praying to the loving God and Savior. Never give up. Never stop praying.

The thread woven throughout these ten ideas is to *live out your faith*. As you grow in your own relationship with God, your husband will notice. He'll recognize the deeper level of love you give, your increased patience, and your acts of kindness. It does no good to try to manipulate, coerce, or badger someone into spiritual intimacy. It won't work. The most effective way to interest a spouse in spiritual matters is to be so attractive in the way you live your life that he simply will feel he must have what you have.

By taking these ten actions you will know that, before God, you've done your absolute best to draw your partner into spiritual intimacy with you.

ASK YOURSELVES THESE QUESTIONS

1. Begin a series of honest talks about the content of this chapter. Using your Couple Talk Times and the "train," share your feelings about your spiritual differences and how they are impacting your relationship.

2. If you're not married, are you willing to break up after six months of trying my strategy? Why would you continue to stay with a partner who does not want to become a Christian or does not want to build a lifelong spiritual bond with you?

3. Which of my ten action steps will be the most difficult for you? Why? Would you explain this to your partner?

4. What do you fear will happen if you follow my strategy?

CHAPTER 23

THE ADVENTURE
BEGINS

CLAMS TEND TO LOVE action-adventure movies. Nonstop thrills and excitement from start to finish. Car chases, car crashes, motorcycle chases, motorcycle crashes, helicopter chases, helicopter crashes, airplane chases . . . well, you get the idea.

Clam movies have an enormous amount of gunfire. Handgun fire, rifle fire, sniper rifle fire, bazooka fire, mortar fire . . . The noise of constant gunfire drowns out dialogue. Oh, wait! That's not a problem because there is no dialogue in the movie.

Actually, there is some dialogue, and usually it's between a man and a woman. Luckily, it is brief and to the point and involves absolutely no romance:

"Hand me my gun."

"Those guys are trying to kill us."

"Help! They're shooting at us."

Crowbars tend to love romantic comedies. Nonstop talking from start to finish. Boy meets girl. They talk and talk. They click. They keep talking. They fall in love. They keep talking. Some dumb mis-understanding occurs, and after a great deal of talking, they break up. They finally stop talking to each other, which is fortunate. But they talk to their best friends about the breakup, which is unfortunate (well, it is if you're a Clam and being forced to watch it). They get back together and . . . continue . . . talking.

The vast majority of the talking is about their relationship. What's great about it, what makes it work, how they feel about each other, how they feel about other relationships they've been in before, how they feel about how these relationships ended, how they feel about their future together, how everything and everyone in their individual lives relates to their relationship . . .

These Crowbar movies have no action, unless you count walking (and talking, of course) in restaurants and on city streets, and in parks and around lakes. There is no gunfire unless you count the rapid-fire words gushing out of the mouths of the two lovers.

I could go on and on about Clams and Crowbars and their prefer-ences in movies. Here's my point: The best movies are those that are a successful combination of action-adventure and romantic comedy. Now that's the best of both worlds! The Clam and the Crowbar can both enjoy this type of movie.

The Best Kind of Marriage

A good marriage is also a combination of action-adventure and romantic comedy. But who wants to settle for a good marriage? A great marriage, the best marriage possible, adds the spiritual factor to the mix. Once you put God at the center of the relationship, you get an action-adventure/romantic comedy directed by God Himself.

In the previous twenty-two chapters, I've shown you how to build a marriage like this. You've learned how to work with your Clam-Crowbar differences to:

- be emotionally intimate through deeper communication
- be able to talk through all difficult topics
- be intimate with God through spiritual bonding

When you've mastered these three skills, you have all you need for the best relationship—whether you are dating or married—you can experience.

You'll have God choreographing everything that happens to you. And He's going to make your life together exciting! You'll have romance and physical passion, because they flow out of emotional and spiritual intimacy. You will have comedy, because instead of driving you crazy, your differences will entertain you and make you laugh.

My Strategy Works!

My strategy has worked for Sandy and me for the past twenty-five years, and it continues to work for us. It has worked for hundreds and hundreds of couples I've seen in therapy. It has worked for hundreds and hundreds of couples who have attended my marriage seminars.

It will work for you and your special person too. Read the book together, apply the principles, and get ready to start living God's adventure for your relationship.

Additional Resources

OTHER BOOKS BY DAVID CLARKE:

Parenting Is Hard and Then You Die: A Fun but Honest Look at Raising Kids of All Ages Right, with William G. Clarke

Kiss Me like You Mean It: Solomon's Crazy in Love How-To Manual

Married but Lonely: Seven Steps You Can Take with or without Your Spouse's Help, with William G. Clarke

I Don't Want a Divorce: A 90-Day Guide to Saving Your Marriage, with William G. Clarke

What to Do When He Says, "I Don't Love You Anymore": An Action Plan to Regain Confidence, Power, and Control

A Marriage after God's Own Heart

I'm Not OK and Neither Are You: The 6 Steps to Emotional Freedom, with William G. Clarke

The Top 10 Most Outrageous Couples of the Bible: And How Their Stories Can Revolutionize Your Marriage, with William G. Clarke

To schedule a seminar, order Dr. Clarke's books, set up an in-person or telephone advice session, schedule a marriage intensive, or access his speaking schedule, please contact:

www.davideclarkephd.com

1-888-516-8844

or

Marriage & Family Enrichment Center

6505 North Himes Avenue

Tampa, Florida 33614

About the Authors

David E. Clarke, Ph.D., is a Christian psychologist and speaker and the author of eleven books, including *Kiss Me like You Mean It, Married but Lonely,* and *I Don't Want a Divorce.* A graduate of Dallas Theological Seminary and Western Conservative Baptist Seminary in Portland, Oregon, he has been in private practice for more than thirty years. He and his wife, Sandy, live in Tampa, Florida, and have four children and three grandchildren.

William G. Clarke, M.A., has been a marriage and family therapist for more than thirty years. He is a graduate of the University of Southern California and the California Family Study Center where he earned his master's degree. With his wife, Kathleen, he served for nine years with Campus Crusade for Christ (now Cru). He is the founder of the Marriage and Family Enrichment Center in Tampa, Florida.